GW00503528

VANISHING TALES FROM ANCIENT TRAILS

(Memoirs from far off the beaten path)
The collected travel essays of James Michael Dorsey

VAGABUNDO MAGAZINE

2014

Copyright ©2014 by Vagabundo Magazine on behalf of James Dorsey

All rights reserved. This book or any portion thereof may not be repro-
duced or used in any manner whatsoever without the express written
permission of the publisher except for the use of brief quotations in a book
review or scholarly journal.

First Printing: August 2014

ISBN 978-1-63443-932-9

Vagabundo Magazine
http://www.vagabundomagazine.com

This book is dedicated to my wife, Irene, who helped to make it all happen and was there with me when most of it did.

"What I like best about James Dorsey's stories is that he tells you not only where he travels, but why he travels. He has an innate ability to coax hidden truths from strangers, to absorb and reflect world cultures without judgment. This remarkable collection of essays allows a reader to share both the external and internal journey of a true adventurer."

- Diane Haithman, Former Staff Writer for the Los Angeles Times, Author of Dark Lady of Hollywood, and also, The Elder Wisdom Circle Guide for a Meaningful Life

FOREWORD
BY
GRAHAM MACKINTOSH

Baja Explorer and author of "Into a Desert Place," winner of the Adventurous Traveler of the Year award.

James Dorsey's collection of travel essays is more than a collection of small untold stories from around the world. With sincerity and humility, Jim takes us to places we will probably never visit and introduces us to people and situations we will likely never know. Thanks to his sensitivity and appreciation for his subjects and his clarity of style, we feel intimately connected to the personal dramas and moments captured in these pages.

Sometimes uplifting, sometimes disturbing, rarely have I moved so effortlessly through a book. As with the author, we may not find the kind of overarching meaning and understanding sought in youthful wanderings, yet in lesser but still important ways we are led to contemplate and, above all, to care… to care about what's being lost forever from the world, and to question our own beliefs, prejudices, and comfort zones.

The author reports on his rickshaw ride around Chau Doc, the northernmost outpost in Vietnam before the Cambodian border, a former United States Special Forces base,

"Our ride lasts about an hour and it has taken us into areas I would not choose to go on my own, yet while on this rickshaw I have felt not only safe, but happy. I have completely left the modern world behind and become the pure traveler, welcomed into stranger's lives because that is the code of the road. If I ever was an enemy, I have now become a friend. We pass each other in the twilight, leaving only the briefest of memories, yet connected by that thread forever."

Upon reading these chapters, especially the one documenting the horrors of Cambodia, a part of me gave thanks for the security and privileges I have enjoyed, but at a deeper level I felt invited, indeed inspired, to reach out, to risk, to step across the divide and make the connections Mr. Dorsey has revealed.

The great age of travel and exploration of our shrinking globe may be over, but the adventure of learning and caring about our fellow travelers still awaits.

AUTHOR'S FOREWORD

In the first century A.D., a Christian mystic named Augustine wrote, "The world is a book, and those who do not travel read only the first page."

I grew up on those words, reading the great works of exploration by the likes of Ernest Shackleton, Roy Chapman Andrews, and Sir Richard Burton, wondering how mortal men could accomplish such epic undertakings, and being years away from even dreaming of following in their footsteps.

Few people remember those names today and their accomplishments have been overshadowed by electronic sound bites that pass for news as each generation creates its own heroes.

The great era of world exploration is over. There are but a few corners of the earth that have not known the tread of a human boot; or at least been recorded from an orbiting camera for future invasion. But there are still hidden places within that realm worth investigating.

A century ago, the great books written by explorers were the evenings' entertainment. Before the internet, television, and even the early days of radio, families would gather by the fireplace to read aloud the epic wanderings of courageous men who went to remote and exotic locales, placing their lives in harms' way in exchange for a life less mundane.

The audience for such books dwindled for a while because the advance of technology had brought with it material comforts that make the pursuit of knowledge, only gained far off the beaten path, less and less appealing all the time. But as one who has attempted to follow in the footsteps of such men, I have sought out the small untold stories, little tales within the great epics that are no less compelling, and are in fact often times more so, as they connect the reader, one on one, with cultural and personal insights that are lost in the major epics.

Today, the term adventure travel represents a multi-billion dollar industry often designed to take affluent city dwellers into remote places for brief periods of time in order to experience adrenalin rushes not normally available to them, but few return with any real knowledge of culture or history of where they have been. Such journeys have become trophies, squeezed into long weekends between 60 hour work weeks. But, while few people have the time or money to experience a major expedition, there is a great resurgence in wanting to know about those who do.

The great travel writer Paul Theroux has said, "Tourists don't know where they have been, and travelers don't know where they are going." But I think it goes deeper than that. Tourists usually journey as a brief respite from lives of repetition while travelers wander to learn. The more I learn, the more I realize what mankind is losing, and how quickly it is vanishing.

Another great writer, anthropologist Wade Davis, has said that on the average, one language passes from this earth each week. That is to say the final speaker of a definitive tongue has ceased to exist forever, and that, to quote an ancient African saying, is "like a library burning."

A language does not die a solo death, but takes an entire culture with it, ending a unique way of life, and slipping from the collective memory of mankind into oblivion. When this happens, it is a global loss.

Mr. Davis estimates there are currently some six thousand languages actively spoken on earth, but a mere century ago there were more than 35,000. Many of these current languages have fewer than a thousand speakers, and even less of them are being passed on to future generations let alone being taught in schools. Imagine the isolation of being the last person of your tribe to speak a language. When that person dies, the world will never know he or she existed, let alone what that world was like.

While I have spent more than three decades wandering in the most remote places I could possibly reach, my intent has always been to sit with an individual and really learn about his or her life while always being aware that a roll of the dice at birth is all that has separated me from the poorest desert nomad or mountain tribesman, and I have, because of that, always asked "What if?"

If I had been born in a mud hut in Ethiopia, the world would never know I existed, but since I have visited mud huts in Ethiopia, I feel compelled to let people know that is how others live. Is there a finer classroom anywhere than sitting with a person of different color, language, beliefs, and ideas, and exchanging such information?

The evolution of a culture is not its death knell, but failure to record that evolution is. How did a person from Africa become different from one in Asia? Without their stories, the world would be very mundane.

Like most naïve young travelers, when I first stepped out that doorway into the vast world, I was full of hopes and dreams, convinced that at some remote time or place a great sadhu or shaman would impart the knowledge of the universe to me as a true seeker. While I learned no great secrets along the way, I do believe I got just a tad wiser with each trip, and have no doubt that many of the people whose stories I collected are much further along the path to enlightenment than I am. People are the same the world over, but it is their stories that make them fascinating.

The stories in this book are not grand tales, but rather personal anecdotes, the likes of which, in a perfect world, should be told among close friends under a crescent moon, far from man-made sounds. These are personal stories that will likely become lost in the fog of time as more and more of our waking hours are spent staring at one sort of electronic screen or another.

As we continue to rely on machines to make our lives better, the impersonality of such pursuits makes us further removed from our fellow man. George Orwell was right, but did not see far enough into the future where the possibility is strong that we will all live within our individual cubicles, communicating only through electronic screens, using numeric codes, sending messages to Ouagadougou or Timbuktu, but having no idea where such places really are or what they are like.

Until you step out the door and physically encounter other lands your information about them can only be superficial. No screen as of yet offers taste, smells, nuance, and imperfection, that give life and meaning to travel.

My journeys have convinced me that the majority of people alive on earth today live in houses made of mud, dung, or cardboard. They have no knowledge of television or a telephone and will not in their lifetime. They do not know what a computer or cell phone is, let alone electricity, and to them an airplane is either a bird or a spirit because nothing else could possibly move about the sky.

These are people whose connection to the earth is beyond the comprehension of those of us who dwell in cities.

After a life of wandering through the most remote places on our planet, I have come to think of myself as a conduit, relating the stories, myths, and legends of those who have no written means of preserving them, to those who have no idea such people or places even exist. Among them, I have added a few of my own that I hope complement those of my hosts.

I am a storyteller, a connector of cultures, and these are my tales.

Each of these stories was written and meant to be read independently so there may be some overlapping of subject matter, and for this I offer an apology, but would rather leave each story in its original form rather than try to force it into the context of a book.

And finally; an acknowledgement.

Many publishers have told me to never write "buddy" travel stories. It makes it difficult for the reader to remember names and is distracting from the storyline. So, while names are mentioned, most of the following stories have been written in the first person. Because of that I wish to acknowledge that accompanying me through various combinations of countries were my brothers from the Explorers Club and The Adventurers Club; Pierre Odier, Alan Feldstein, Michael Gwaltney, Ken Freund, Dr. Rosaly Lopes and Karen Tate.

TALES FROM ASIA

A MAGIC RICKSHAW RIDE

Boats appear like spirits through the mist, and a velvety morning haze coats the Mekong River creating a gauze curtain between the jungle and us.

In a shoreline eddy, I watch a boil of catfish compete for breakfast, and the sunrise, filtered through a thousand coal fires, blurs all the edges, as though we are sailing through an impressionist painting.

On this, our third day of chugging northward from Saigon, our tiny boat pulls into Chau Doc, the northernmost outpost in Vietnam before the Cambodian border.

During the time known locally as the "American" war, this little village was a United States Special Forces base charged with operating heavily armed river patrol boats. Although I did not fight in that war, I am the age to have done so, and am apprehensive that the locals may view me as a returning soldier, chasing memories or maybe ghosts. With my wife, Irene, on this trip, I am even more paranoid.

In the large suburban centers such as Hanoi and Saigon, I was courteously received as a wealthy tourist adding to the economy, but here in this speck of a jungle hamlet I have no such expectations. Chau Doc had once been the eye of the storm.
How do these people treat former enemies? Until I know, I shall keep a low profile. This is only a stop on our way into Cambodia. Irene and I will slip over the border in the morning, then disappear into the jungle, here only for an evening's rest and a hot meal.

As our boat docks at the Hotel Victoria, the grandeur of the French colonial past stands in stark contrast to the recent neon and glass offerings of modern developers who have moved into the south like so many post war carpetbaggers. Today's Ho Chi Minh City with its steel high rises could be any city in Asia, but Chau Doc is still Indochina.

A beautiful young lady in traditional Au-Dai shuffles down to greet us with an ice cold glass of water tinged with lime and places a lei of flowers around our necks as she kisses our cheeks. I am embarrassed by my stench after a day under the relentless river sun. She must notice my smell but pretends not to.

A uniformed doorman snaps to attention as our sweaty entourage passes inside between two sandstone lion deities whose job it is to prevent bad joss from following us.

Our lady guides us to the registration desk where two immaculately groomed Khmer bow and greet us in accented English. The opulence of this aging hotel only accentuates the extreme poverty of the masses directly outside its polished doors. It is a monument to a time long past and will be almost like spending the night in a museum.

Inside our room, geckos dot the walls like refrigerator magnets, a constant reminder that this is Southeast Asia. I turn on the ceiling fan and watch them scurry as I step onto the balcony into the blast furnace heat of the afternoon.
The sun is a swirling orange ball that steals my vision for a moment. Then I begin to see silhouettes of the churning mass on the streets. This village is alive and moving as I would only expect to see in a much larger city.

Directly below us are the contingent of resident beggars, detritus of the war with my country; legless and armless men forced to rely on the pity of a trickle of tourists passing through this remote village. These are the men who should hate me.

A sea of bicycles fills the street, and the smell of trash, sun baked fish, and unwashed bodies remind me I am only separated from this by the chance of birth. For me, third world travel has always been the finest antidote to the arrogance of American materialism.

The local rickshaw drivers spot me and begin to congregate below my balcony yelling up offers of cheap rides and more intimate offers should I desire them.
Looking left and right I see there are no other bodies in sight, only vacant balconies, and realize we may be the only white people for many miles. Only tourists can afford this hotel and right now it appears to be empty except for us. Irene joins me outside, and this rare spectacle is now attracting a crowd. We step back inside and Irene asks, why not go out and

see what happens? At the moment, she feels more adventurous than I do.

Downstairs in the lobby, we pass two aging, rumpled Frenchmen playing Backgammon under a veil of Galois smoke.

How do I know they are French? Their essence is unmistakable; former masters who have lost everything, victims of regime change; barflies who live off a small pension, who can no longer afford to return home, and after decades in the jungle are too native to want to. The "March or Die" tattoo on ones' hand labels him an ex Para, if not a legionnaire.

In Bangkok such men are expatriate American soldiers, but here in Vietnam, they are all French. Such men were once professional soldiers or plantation owners. After the war they were probably mercenaries, but now, most that I have encountered are just drunks, passing through the remainder of their lives in a smoky haze.

No sooner are we on the dirt street than we are mobbed, not just by rickshaw drivers but the general populace. In this part of town, many of the people are well clothed but there is also a fair number of tattered poor among them. What are lacking here are the beggars. They keep their station outside the hotel, lurking in the shadows, while not one person in this crowd asks for money. These people are curious, pushing inward as if proximity will reveal hidden secrets.

One man asks in English, "Soldier? When I say no he seems disappointed. We smile and bow, making our way to the nearest rickshaw. As the driver assists Irene onto the high seat, I see he has gained great face as her choice. Since I am large, I decide to take a separate rickshaw hoping not to overburden these wiry little men with my occidental girth. There is much laughter as this tiny man attempts to help lift me up onto his ride. I pretend to struggle and the crowd eats it up.

As my driver strains to peddle a weight he is unaccustomed to, people begin to close in and touch my clothing. Most of them say, "Hello" in accented English that tells me this is the only word of the language they know, yet it is said in a sincerely friendly manner.

Our tiny convoy picks up speed and Irene turns to take a picture of me. This seems very funny to our followers who begin to laugh and clap their hands. We are suddenly minor celebrities and everyone is having a good time. The drivers turn up a side street, taking us out of the central area and into private residences where word has preceded us, and I notice folks coming out of their houses as we have become a parade with people lining the street, all waving and yelling "Hello" as we pass. Many stick out a hand for a quick shake or simply to touch mine as we glide by.

Several barking dogs have joined us adding to the carnival atmosphere and many young children run alongside, yelling and laughing, high fiving as we pass, then race forward to do so again and again. One young boy streaks ahead like a scout, repeatedly yelling, "Mericans"

Elders laugh from toothless mouths and wave from their porch chairs. Some young women giggle and hide their faces behind a hand as I pass, while most of the men stare openly at Irene. We are both a diversion and a curiosity, and most surely the biggest event to hit this neighborhood in some time.

We weave in and out of dark muddy streets, tasting of rural life that most visitors will never see. Stone and plaster houses stand side by side with cardboard shacks. In the fading light, candles and an occasional gas lantern begin to cast eerie shadows. The smell of grease, fish, and sweat lingers on the air, and I take it all in with a pilgrims' gratitude.

As the sun begins to sink, lingering smoke from hundreds of charcoal fires blurs the light and turns the swirling ball a red reminiscent of Van Gogh. One little pig is almost run over by our tires and he scurries into the tall grass squealing in terror to the delight of our groupies. A small boy tosses a piece of sugar cane onto my lap and stands waving as I disappear from his life. I could easily have been born that young boy and been the one throwing sugar cane at the rich giant from the land of plenty, when it hits me how lifes' simple paradoxes always seem to come to me at these moments.

My driver is covered with sweat from his labor and I can see the tendons of his back straining under his wet T-shirt with Che Guevara glaring back at me. Hauling me through this heat is a major task, yet he repeatedly turns to smile at me through beetle nut stained teeth, happy to be part of the spectacle. I turn to see Irene's driver, a cigarette dangling from his ear to ear smile, waving as if he himself were responsible for all this entertainment.

Our ride lasts about an hour and it has taken us into areas I would not choose to go on my own, yet while on this rickshaw I have felt not only safe, but happy. I have completely left the modern world behind and become the pure traveler, welcomed into strangers' lives because that is the code of the road. If I ever was an enemy, I have now become a friend. We pass each other in the twilight, leaving only the briefest of memories, yet connected by that thread forever.

It is moments like this that keep pulling me back to the road less traveled; moments that at the time seem insignificant, but in the fog of hindsight take on great importance as the point of connection between peoples whose paths would normally never cross. This ride filled my soul with frozen moments that will reside there until death.

Arriving back at the hotel, we bow to our drivers and I pay them three times their asking price. This amounts to a couple of dollars but gives both them, and us, great face.

There is sporadic applause as Irene and I wave goodbye and disappear into our other world that is beyond the dreams of most of the people we have just encountered.

Up in our room, I peek through the curtains and see an animated crowd below discussing the evenings' events and feel good to have given these people a story that will grow larger with each retelling.

In such rural villages, storytelling has long been a valued art. I have now passed from a mere traveler into a story, and by doing so, I leave part of myself here when I go.

The thought makes me smile.

THE JEWEL OF BENG MELEA

Soukhouen tells me to step only where he does and I don't need to be told twice.

The deaths heads on either side of the trail are content to wait, knowing sooner or later they will claim another victim.

Steam, rising from the morning dew under a blistering sun, blankets everything in an eerie, horror movie ground fog, crawling across the jungle floor, then begins to climb the tumbled granite blocks that have witnessed two thousand years of war.

The scattered temple of Beng Melea is the ancient soul of Cambodia, a silent monolith of memories, in the clinging grasp of a predatory jungle, and 30 years after the last bullet was fired in anger it is still saturated with land mines.

This is our first stop on a journey through time to follow a story about persecution, degradation, and ultimately about perseverance and renewal.

In this country where one out of every six people follows the religious path, the history of Theravada Buddhism is intertwined with that of the nation. It is the veins and arteries that pump the lifeblood through a war torn nation buried by poverty, and it is the story of those who wear the saffron robes; one of the most epic survival tales in history.

Soukhoeun, unlike most Khmer men, had not spent time as a monk, but knew their true stories could only be found deep in the jungle, at isolated villages and temples where the survivors of the last great horror have chosen to end their physical days away from the distractions of their fellow man.

Why the Khmer empire vanished no one knows for sure, but war has a way of wearing civilizations down, and my boot prints follow those of countless armies who have bled into this land; but always, in the end, the jungle returns to hide the sins of mankind. At Beng Melea, it is so quiet, personal imagination supplies the soundtrack of human conflict. At this killing field, the cries of lost souls are deafening. It has suffered invasions from China, Thailand, France, America, and Vietnam, while the entire history and mythology of a people, carved in stone, standing silent watch, has born witness to it all.

During all of these wars, monks were an easy and logical target and they died in waves, but it was only during this lifetime that they came from the edge of extinction.

The ruins of Beng Melea are a mere 65 kilometers east, but a thousand years removed, from Siem Reap, the once quiet village that is now the neon capitol of Cambodian towns, and gateway to the trashy tourist stalls that infect Angkor Wat. While Angkor sits atop the tourist heap with millions of annual visitors, Beng Melea is known only to those intrepid few who venture far off the beaten path, a window to a vanished culture, that in its day produced some of the finest artisans the world had known and a flourishing civilization that raised magnificent cities while that of my own country was living in nomadic shelters.

For centuries, Beng Melea has only given up its past in bits and pieces. It is the least visited and least explored temple in the nation. The Khmer people avoid it, thinking it a spirit land of lost souls. In a country where one out of six people is a victim of a landmine, Beng Melea has claimed more than its share. There are no plans to restore it, because there is simply no money, but for this I am grateful, because to me she is a far more attractive ruin with all the years upon her.

Begun in the late 11th century and finished early in the 12th, Beng Melea predates its showier cousin by over a century and is believed to be the model on which the main temples of Angkor were modeled. Satellite imagery has revealed a wagon wheel of roads emanating from its center in all directions, proving it once linked the entire Khmer empire, and stood as the hub of its activity. Its lush jungle has tasted the blood of soldiers from six nations while knowing only 40 years of real peace in the past two millenniums.

During the "American" war, in jungles too thick for the insertion of infantry, ground penetrating land mines were "carpet" dropped over hundreds of miles, and now here I am, four decades later, trying not to step on one.

The drive there, although short, is brutal, on a road punctuated by old artillery strikes and countless military checkpoints, some authentic, some freelance, but all with heavily armed men demanding money that goes directly into the pockets of local generals. These are the same men who were once lieutenants under Pol Pot and the Khmer Rouge. They still run the country but now have fancier uniforms.

Bouncing over potholes and waiting for the shriek of snapping steel as our axle gives up the ghost, I am taken by the smoke from countless wood fires that blanket the forest, softening all the edges and filtering the velvety yellow morning sunlight, giving a false sense of peace and tranquility.

We pass a car, an ancient Rambler sedan with no windows and apparently no engine. It is harnessed to a water buffalo with reins running back across the hood and into the cab where eight people ride with another four sitting on the roof. It is a jungle taxi and the only vehicle we see all day.

At one rickety guardhouse a soldier with an aging AK47 demands $2 US. I am out of singles and offer him a $5 bill in hopes it may buy us some good will along with a pass. He holds it up to the light and tugs on it hard as though he would know counterfeit, and I stifle a smile when he leans his rifle against the car and reaches into his pocket to give me back $3 in change that he pulls from a wad of dollars and euros.

The road ends at a marshy bog imprinted by the large round feet of an adult elephant, which in turn, has left behind a steaming pile of dung for the flies. Another soldier takes a dollar to guard our car. I know I am paying him not to rob us, but he will probably do so anyway.

One constant at these remote sites is the children. These are the leftovers of the slaughtered innocents, the detritus of war. Some are second generation, homeless born and bred, but still orphans none the less, with no skills, education, or hope of getting either, so they linger near the temple entrances in hopes of preying on the guilt of visiting tourists for a few coins. Some hold photos of long dead relatives. They are a sad fact of life in Cambodia, too numerous to help, and too pitiful to ignore. Their skeletal appearance reveals the small number of visitors they receive, and I distribute my day's supply of beef jerky among them, like adding a drop of water to the ocean. The trail takes us past a seven headed Naga, the ubiquitous temple guardian of a giant multi headed cobra that flanks the main pathway. This one has been shot to pieces and try as I might I am unable to pry an aging rifle round from one bullet hole.

We pass massive webs with spiders larger than my fist. The morning dew still clings to their webs, catching sparks of sunlight through the jungle canopy and sending prisms dancing on the occasional breeze. I stop to wonder why battlefields always seem so beautiful to me.

When the path disappears into bush and Soukhouen starts to swing his machete, I grab his belt, walking close enough behind him to plant my feet only where his have gone and flinching at the snap of every twig.

After a few yards he leans against a banyan tree and tells me he had been at this very spot only one month prior on a picnic with his wife and small son. He felt something poking him in the rear that turned out to be an anti-tank mine. He did not weigh enough to detonate it. The tree is in the middle of the current safe zone. He says this with a small laugh as only one who lives close to death can.

I know and trust Soukhouen because he had brought me here a year prior to photograph the ruins. Standing in the central courtyard atop a jumbled pile of granite blocks, I dropped my camera's memory card and watched it slide into the black depths into a maze of ancient granite blocks and sleeping cobras.

With my heart stopped, Soukhouen went into action, and without me hearing or seeing anything, people began to materialize out of the jungle. He called them somehow through that silent jungle telegraph that only animals and those who dwell within can hear, and they gathered to help me, a stranger they would never see again. They came simply because they were asked.

Women burned incense and chanted, invoking Buddha, while men shouldered giant stone blocks under a blazing sun, sliding them inches at a time, moving tons of rock with nothing but sinewy arms and legs, while I prayed that two weeks' worth of photos would return to me.

They labored for hours, and in the end, could not retrieve my card, but by that time I no longer cared. I had been given a far more valuable gift. I had watched these amazing people labor all day in brutal heat and humidity. None of them knew what a memory card was and it did not matter anyway. They came for no other reason than a stranger needed help, expecting nothing in return.

This is the spirit of Beng Melea. It is people like this that make a civilization great, and in that moment, the nature of Buddhism had been revealed to me. I realized I was not meant to retrieve that card. It was now a time capsule, waiting for some distant date in the future to give up its secrets, while I was but a spectator of this great drama. Instant karma.

A hand on my arm brings me out of my reverie. An old man has appeared at my side. He is just there, like a spirit with a wispy beard. He takes my arm as I descend, and though he is holding me up, his touch is as light as an implication.

At first I think he wants money, but Soukhouen reminds me it was this same man who came to my aid almost a year ago to the day. He is beaming at me through a one tooth smile the color of beetle nut, happy that I now remember him.

On that day he had bowed and offered me the clasp handed Khmer greeting, refusing my money while telling Soukhouen he had lost face for not having retrieved my memory card, and before I could add a word, he turned and disappeared into the jungle. I thought about this man throughout that night and many more since then, wondering if I could ever be that good a person.

I have returned because of that card. Not just to reshoot the lost images but to relive those perfect moments of mankind at its humble best. The little man will not leave my side, determined to see I have no more mishaps on his watch. He leads me over the jumbled stones, pointing where I should step while spitting long streams of beetle nut juice.

There is no one else here. Soukhouen has gone off to pray, and I am alone with my silent shadow who I accept as a guardian angel. We have no common words with which to communicate and none are needed. When I look at him he smiles, and my day becomes as good as it gets.

I move stealthily through the tangled puzzle of rock and jungle, willing there to be no cobras. Wherever I look a photo presents itself and all I have to do is press the shutter. At the end of the day, the wonder of Beng Melea lies safely within my camera once again. I have gained all the photos I lost, and much more. Half of me wants to tell the world about this place, and half wants it to stay hidden.

I sit on a tree root sorting through money, trying to decide a fit reward to give my little shadow for this wonderful day, but when I look up, I see his back disappearing into the undergrowth. He took no money then, and he will take none now. He has come into my life at two critical moments and disappeared as soon as they were resolved, a phantom I could not have created for a fictional story. I feel a life bond with him and he has hardened my belief that at certain times in our lives a cosmic plan kicks in regardless of what we believe or do.

In the late afternoon, covered with mud, Soukhouen and I find our car intact with the guard sitting on the hood, and I am so grateful I give him another dollar that he accepts with a shocked look.

Soukhouen and I tumble inside, drenched in sweat and exhausted. He gives me a tiny smile and whispers, "Cambodia."

A MONK'S TALE

Backlit by the sunrise, the silhouetted spires of Angkor Wat probe for the sky like fingers of a deity.

These temples, the soul of the Khmer nation, are too gorgeous a backdrop for the tale of horror I have come to record.

I see Pan approaching, fingering his prayer beads, his saffron robes seemingly ablaze in the yellow mist. He walks as though he is not really there, feet barely touching the ground, a saint incarnate to the world at large but in his own eyes, a simple humble monk.

He is bent from time and suffering, having lived through and seen more than anyone should, and I know through mutual friends he wishes nothing more than to spend his remaining time in secluded meditation, but upon hearing of my book project he readily agreed to speak with me in the hopes that no one should have to relive it.

Pan is a Theravada monk, one of about 350,000 throughout Cambodia prior to the Khmer Rouge, and now one of but 30 to have outlived their regime. Besides surviving personal atrocities, he bears the weight of trying to re-establish a religious order dragged to the brink of extinction under their barbaric reign.

Theravada means, "Teaching of the Elders." It is one of three main branches of Buddhism that originated in northern India and Nepal in the sixth century B.C. and rapidly spread throughout Southeast Asia until it was introduced to Cambodia in the 13th century via monks from Sri Lanka. It is a personal religion that worships no deity but rather teaches self-control in order to release all attachment to the material world and achieve personal enlightenment. Most Khmer men spend time as a novice before deciding to take the saffron robes or return to a secular life. For many it is the only escape from a life of dire poverty and only hope for at least a minimal education. For Pan, it was a calling that put him in the eye of the storm.

The reign of the Khmer Rouge has been likened to a shark attack, increasing in speed and fury, feeding upon its own momentum as more and more blood is spilled. In the headlong rush to turn Cambodia into a submissive, agrarian, socialist state, it was the Buddhist monks who bore the brunt of the assault.

Their modest education made them a threat to the powers that be and since they do not work in the traditional sense of the word, they were easily made into the national whipping boy, publicly declared useless and a drain on society that needed to be removed.

Pan sits next to me on the stone railing of the Angkor moat bridge, lightly as a butterfly landing, radiating peace. He has come to tell his tale and begins by opening an old oil cloth to reveal a small, shiny bowl; his rice bowl as he calls it.

In a matter of fact voice he tells me it is the top of his brother's skull, killed by the Khmer Rouge, and in true Buddhist fashion, he has kept it as a daily reminder of his own frailty and impermanence. He stares at his dangling sandaled feet, too short to reach the ground, as he speaks. There is no self-pity or even regret in his voice. To him it is all karma, and all that surrounds him now is but Maya, an illusion to wander through until he reaches true enlightenment.

His story begins with the first night, when he was still a novice and was lighting candles around the monastery when the door burst in and everyone was herded out at gunpoint. Outside, in a huddled mass the Abbott and all elders were singled out and summarily shot with a single bullet to the back of the head. By now, the attendant nuns were being stripped by the soldiers, intent on a long night of debauchery.

Next he tells me several monks were hung in the trees by their thumbs with small fires built underneath them, not enough to kill but just large enough to singe the skin. One of the nuns, who was by now hysterical, was stripped, held down, and a monk was made to kneel between her knees. A pistol was put to his head and he was ordered to copulate with her in front of all present. When he refused, a single shot rang out to the applause and cheers of the "soldiers" and another monk was brought forward. According to Pan, this went on for quite a while, until several monks had done the deed while several more had died in refusing.

I search his face at this point for some sign, some emotional reaction, but see only tranquility. His roadmap face is a spider web of creases but his eyes burn bright. I pray his religious advancement had brought him true peace and that he is not simply numb in relating such unspeakable events. He returns my stare with a slight smile and says, "Tell this story once so it might never be told a second time."

We begin to walk into the main courtyard of Angkor and though surrounded by thousands of tourists, I hear only Pan as he continues in his soft voice.

He was sent to the countryside and made to rip up railroad tracks, brutally physical work under a blazing sun while enduring non-stop blows from the fists and whips of his overseers. Soon, near starvation, and with only putrid river water to drink, he was near death, the final plan for him from the beginning. In the end, his will to live overcame his belief in karma as he crawled away one night, into the jungle, and there, lost all track of time.

He was not sure how long he stayed in the jungle, but once there he soon found others like himself, survivors, all with an unspeakable story, all wishing to live. Everyone had a talent, some could fish, others snared small animals; Pan knew a lot about medicinal plants and soon became a gypsy doctor, moving every few days, avoiding roads and villages, helping the more needy for a handful of rice, defying the odds at the bottom of the food chain.

One day, while foraging near a village he spotted a saffron robe and, not believing his eyes, knew he had to talk with this brother. The Khmer Rouge were gone but the damage had been done. Pan listened to the monk's litany of atrocities all day but told me he fell asleep while doing so and the next morning, he woke up under a roof, on a cot, for the first time in months if not years.

When he revealed his identity, he was called to the capitol of Phnom Penh where he was received as a revered elder and met a delegation of Theravada monks from Vietnam who had come to help re-establish the religion. Only then did he realize the extent of the genocide, the monasteries destroyed, the sacred texts burned, countless brother monks slaughtered, and for the only time in our conversations, I saw a single tear roll down his cheek.

Two subsequent visits with Pan were deliberately kept light hearted and fun, and I learned that he loved shave ice and to laugh, but it is more of a sustained giggle than a laugh that spares no part of his face. His joy in all that surrounded him reminded me of a small child and though I could not see it, I often felt his aura.

When I left, Pan was in great demand, traveling around to various monasteries, imparting the old ways, "The Teaching of the Elders" to a new generation of monks who now used the internet, had cellphones and IPods, and ride motorbikes, but this did not seem to bother him in the least; how could it? Karma.

His goal had always been to spend his life in meditation and I am sure that since our time together he has merged with the cosmos. I have allowed myself the fantasy to think he may have been looking over my shoulder as I wrote this and would know that his story had been told, one more time, for the last time.

Today there are close to 60,000 Theravada monks throughout the country and almost 5,000 monasteries, all because men like Pan refused to give up their faith, and though he would laugh and shake his head at the thought, he is one who made a difference.

WHAT'S IN A WORD?

Winston Churchill once said the Americans and British are two peoples separated by a common language. The more countries I visit, the more this seems to be true around the globe.

For better or worse, English has become the second language for most of the world. While no one cause can be singled out for this, I believe there are two great contributing factors.

First, after World War Two, we were one of two superpowers left standing. Since we stood for freedom and democracy while the other guys represented repression and submission, it only made sense for folks to want to talk to us. Second, in the 1950's when commercial air travel started to become affordable and popular, it quickly became obvious how hard it would be to land in New York or Los Angeles when the pilots spoke only Farsi or Japanese. An international conference was held to decide an official language for the airlines and the world chose English.

All that aside, I never cease to be amazed by people who speak impeccable English in the mountains of Peru or the jungles of Cambodia. English has spread around the globe more effectively than swine flu. But, I have found that an accent can be quite an obstacle.

Irene and I were with a friend in the tiny town of Battambang in central Cambodia. We hired a guide to take us up the river to our next destination at Siem Reap. This was to be a six-hour trip followed by crossing Lake Sap, the largest lake in Central Asia.

Battambang is an extremely poor area, and our mode of transport was a very small and battered boat, not much larger than the four of us. It showed much sign of repair and of course, it was open to the elements.

With six bags lashed to the bow, three travelers and the boatman, I figured we were overloaded by at least a ton. We frequently had seen four or five people on a single motorbike in Cambodia so no one but us was concerned about our weight or its distribution.

We had been on the water only a few minutes when our pilot made for shore and hopped from our boat to another. Our guide said not to worry; he would only be a minute. He then added, "We need to pick up live chickens for their legs."

Irene and I exchanged glances. We are pretty open-minded, especially when traveling in the third world. It was obvious there was little room in our tiny vessel for live chickens. If we had to take them along, we were willing to hold them on our laps as there was no place else to put them. The thought even occurred to me that perhaps the chickens were needed if the boat's single engine stopped in the middle of nowhere.

I had a vision of us holding them over the side while their tiny legs paddled away, guiding us to safety. After all, our guide said we needed them for their legs.

We proceeded to make numerous jokes about live chickens towing us to shore if we capsized or about eating them if we became marooned in the jungle. Meanwhile, the pilot returned with a pile of floatation vests but no fowl.

Puzzled by this Irene turned to him and asked, "How many chickens are we taking?"

At first he seemed totally bewildered by this question, and then as he caught on a large smile spread over his face and he began to laugh Irene said, "I'm glad he thinks us holding live chickens on our laps for six hours is funny." When he finished laughing, he looked at us and very loudly enunciated, "No live chickens! What I said was, "We need life jackets for the lake!"

It took a moment for this to sink in. "Life jackets for the lake" when filtered through a Cambodian accent, came to my ears as "Live chickens for their legs." Suddenly we all found this to be profoundly funny and in fact for the next six hours chicken jokes abounded as we threw our life jackets about while making clucking sounds.

Whenever we made eye contact, our guide would laugh; shake his head and say, "Americans are so funny."

ONE NIGHT IN SAIGON

Our flight landed at Tan Son Nhut international at 10:00 p.m. and we were tired.

Saigon is a great city, and like most old Asia hands, I refuse to call it Ho Chi Minh City. To me it will always be Saigon. It is an exhilarating city, but this time I was just passing through, mission accomplished.

It had been a hard 16 days, going up the Mekong by small boat, then into the Cambodian jungle, but we had the photos in the can and it was time to go home. Pierre and I felt good about the work we had done, got all the shots we were after, and now I looked forward to curling up with a book in the lounge for our 14-hour layover.

We cruised up to the transit counter and handed over our passports, a formality before entering the duty free world of Belgian chocolates and Cuban Cigars that were calling my name after two weeks of rice and Nan.

The smiling face behind the counter suddenly looked grim as she said, "Your visas have expired."

I stepped forward with my most conciliatory grin and said, "I know, but we are just transiting through the airport and don't need visas." We had gotten single entry visas for our initial entrance to the country two weeks prior and they expired the day before knowing that transient passengers did not need them while staying in the airport.

She asked for our tickets and then informed us that our flight left the following day, 14 hours from now. When I acknowledged this she said that is not transiting and directed us to a seat. She told us we would have to talk with immigration authorities and put us under several hot lights where we were left to fidget for the next hour.

Pierre says we should have gotten multiple entry visas, and I reply it never occurred to me, as it is not necessary to have one while in transit. The problem of the moment being our interpretation of transiting and the

Vietnamese officials' version do not match up.

After an hour a tall intense fellow in a bad suit shows up and in perfect English says, "Tell me your story." I explain to him we have flown in from Siem Reap Cambodia and simply wanted to crash in the airport lounge for 14 hours until our flight to Taiwan leaves the next day. He rubs his face with an 'I've heard it all before" gesture and squints at me through the harsh light.

He informs us that a 14 hour layover taking place on two separate days is not transiting and so we must leave the airport, but we cannot leave the airport without a visa, Catch 22. I wonder if he has ever read Joe Heller?

Pierre shoots me one of those 'I'm going to kill you" looks because I had assumed pre-trip responsibilities of getting all necessary paperwork taken care of.

Mr. Bad suit tells us to sit tight and he will see what he can do, then disappears with our passports, and we sit for another hour. Several people with various uniforms stroll by acting casual but obviously wishing to see the two curious Americans.

When he returns he is smiling. I am instantly on guard because I know a cobra smiles just before it strikes.

"Tell you what I'm going to do." he says. "Technically you are in transit but if you stay here you become a security risk. Security tells me anyone here longer than four hours is loitering and rounds them up, it's your 911 you know" he says with a shrug, as if 911 was something unique to Americans.

He says he is going to send us to a tourist hotel in the city, even pick up the tab for the ride, but we will have to pay for the hotel. He gives me a name to see at immigration the following morning to pick up our passports and says we are not to leave the hotel for any reason. If we do so, we are illegal aliens with no papers.

Pierre starts to say something about not leaving without his passport, but I give him an elbow. This is a good deal and we are in no position to argue. Not only are we going to sleep in a bed rather than on a hard airport seat, but also they are providing transport to do so. I will worry about passports in the morning.

We are turned over to an immigration officer who glares at us all the way to the baggage carousel where we pick up our luggage. I avoid eye contact thinking he is just looking for any excuse. He eyes us up and down as we walk and I guess he is thinking we are arrogant Americans for traveling with no papers when suddenly he says in perfect English, "What are you shooting?"

Suddenly we are talking photography in the middle of the airport lobby with Mr. hard cop who has become one big smile.

All around us the limo drivers jockey for position with their name signs. "Mr. and Mrs. Sturat, w/Travel Indochina." "Mr. R Holcomb, w/Saigon Hilton." Suddenly one of these drivers is next to us with his sign asking if Pierre and I are Mr. and Mrs. Anderson. I laugh and tell him no. Mr. Immigration cop is telling us about his Nikon when the driver returns and asks again if we are Mr. and Mrs. Anderson. He does not seem to know or realize one of his clients is supposed to be a woman. He is convinced it is us and we are avoiding him.

A young man stands close beside me while his wife or girlfriend quickly snaps our photo as if we are old friends. He throws me a quick little bow and scurries away giggling.

The gender confused driver is now arguing with our escort and is ordered away by the official just as our car arrives. There is a bellman from the hotel in full livery complete with white gloves, who takes our bags. The immigration man orders the crowd to part and suddenly we have gone from being stateless fugitives to government escorted VIP's. A flash bulb goes off in my face and a crowd gathers around us. I wonder what fabricated story will appear with it in the morning papers?

As we wade through the sea of people we are instant celebrities, and Pierre begins to smile and wave like some rock star. He is enjoying this way too much.

The driver holds the door open and our bags go into the boot as people crowd around to see the American celebrities who have a government escort to their car. For a final touch, the immigration man salutes us as we ride away into the Saigon night.

At the hotel the bellman is looking through a stack of papers on his lap then turns to me and says, "So you are here illegally and need refuge for the night. I will take care of you." He reminds me of Peter Lorrie in a black and white movie, and that is no comfort.

The hotel is clean but in a seedy part of town. The lobby is full of western faces and I wonder how many are here like us, because of some political oversight or simply as tourists.

The bellman hands our passport to the check in clerk who glances at us with a smirk. Obviously our story has preceded us and he is amused by his illegal guests.

Our room is awash with flashing neon even through thick blackout curtains. One look up and down the block tells me we are in the red light district.

Pierre is worried about our passports and cannot sleep so we head for the cafe and a few beers.

Once in the cafe Pierre picks up a hotel ad for massage and asks the waiter if it is too late to get one. "No Problem" he replies, anything we want. It is almost midnight now and I think the masseuse will be off duty. The waiter returns with our beers and asks for our room number then asks what sort of girl Pierre wants.

Finally it hits us what he is talking about. We pay for the beers and retire to our neon filled room. I look out the window and see a state police officer looking up at our balcony and think it is no coincidence.

In the morning the same bellman takes us back to the airport, walks with us to immigration where we pick up our passports and head for the transit lounge.

At the same counter where all this began the evening before, we present our passports to the official on duty who looks up at us and says, "Your visas have expired."

THE SILENT ARMY

The army stands in place, nearly 7000 strong. Arrayed in battle formation, unmoving; not even blinking; they are a juggernaut about to pounce. Each face is unique; a study in concentration of warriors ready to die.

The commanding general and his aides ride chariots behind armor shrouded horses. Legions of archers, lancers and foot soldiers surround them. A sense of doom pervades the air. War is about to be unleashed.

Most amazingly, this army lived 2500 years ago.

We have braved the summer monsoons of central China, traveling to Xian in a pelting downpour. I welcome the cooling rain after the sweltering humidity of Beijing, knowing three dozen people have died in the floods. This is the normal state of affairs for China in summer. We spend most of an afternoon sitting next to an underwater highway, watching military engineers attempt to pump away an inland sea of rainwater. They wave me off when I attempt to take photos.

Discretion must be used when taking pictures in China. The military must look its best, and they do not like being seen doing manual labor. Our driver passes the day chain-smoking Marlboros and cursing the weather. I tell him we will wait all day if necessary. He smiles at this through a cloud of smoke. We are here to see the Terra Cotta Army of Emperor Qin.

In 259 BC, China was a series of feuding states commanded by local warlords all calling themselves "King." That year, the wife of the "King" of Qin province bore a son, Zhao Zheng. When the boy was 13 his father died and he ascended the local throne, changing his name to Ying Zheng. Being too young to govern, his mother administered the affairs of state till the boy reached the age of 22. At that time he began a series of military conquests to unite the various provinces. In 221 BC, at the age of 39, he had defeated the six ruling warlords and united the country, declaring himself to be "Qin Shi Huang Di," First Emperor of Qin.

Today he is known as Emperor Qin, and the modern state of China claims its name from him. Emperor Qin suffered a lifelong fear of death. He constantly searched for an elixir to guarantee his immortality. Having failed to find one, he decided to assure himself an easy passage into the hereafter by taking his legions with him. He amassed an army of artisans almost as large as his military. He commanded them to create a life-size clay duplicate of every soldier in his service. One by one his soldiers modeled for the sculptors. As each statue was finished, it was fired in a kiln, painted, and mounted in a giant pit, exactly where that man would stand in formation on a battlefield. When they finished, the emperor had a terra cotta duplicate of his entire army.

Qin died, at the age of 50. The next Emperor ordered all of Qin's concubines who had not born him children put to death and interred with him. The thousands of artisans who created this wonder were also put under the sword, to assure it remained a secret to the outer world. For 2,400 years, the army stood silent and unknown, covered in its tomb next to the Emperor himself. In 1974 a poor farmer named Yang Jun Peng dug a water well for his village. Breaking into a dark cavern, he found small pieces of metal and shards of terra cotta. At first he was disgusted at not finding water and tossed the pieces away. A village elder realized the importance of his find and notified local authorities. Four months later a massive excavation began. No one was prepared for what they would find.

Two thousand years of earthquakes, floods, and a fire had taken its toll. Most of the army was in small pieces. Still, the sheer size of the discovery dictated a massive effort on the government's part. Museum curators and restorers were dispatched to begin assembling the world's largest jigsaw puzzle.

By 1979, more than 1,000 warriors had been reassembled, plus 300 horses and dozens of chariots. A massive museum complex was constructed to house the army and its restoration. In 1987, UNESCO declared the area a World Heritage Site.

The current army finally lowers the flood waters enough for us to creep through, and we slip and slide into the parking lot. I see two buses unloading their cargo of saffron-robed monks. As each one disembarks, they immediately open identical white umbrellas. Arm in arm they scurry into the building like a moving garden of mushrooms. I follow them inside, snapping their photos and amusing them greatly. The first look at the army is overwhelming. They occupy an enormous pit inside a building the size of an airline hangar. It is dark inside, for daylight can damage these delicate pieces.

Most of the warriors are over six feet tall; some are close to seven. These soldiers were recruited from northern Mongolian stock and were formidable in size. The statues tower over modern-day Chinese. The detail is astonishing. Each piece of armor is articulated. Mustaches, beards, hairstyles, even fingernails are rendered with exacting craftsmanship. Archers wear silk scarves to swivel their necks without rubbing them raw on leather gauntlets. Boot soles have ripples. Thongs wrap around leggings so they will not catch the brush while on the march. Hair is tied to one side, allowing a clear draw of an arrow from back quivers. Horsemen have spurs and infantrymen wear body armor. Horses wear leather jerkins to ward off arrows and blinders to keep them moving forward. If a piece of equipment existed in the actual army, it was faithfully recreated.

Row after row of combatants stand in silent formation, awaiting their orders. It is more than daunting to stare into faces that lived and fought more than two millennia ago. Every statue is unique. Each is the death mask of its owner. Visitors do not speak here. Partly out of reverence, but even more, it is the unconscious longing to hear the order for battle being called. At any moment the march will begin. This army is alive.

In 2002 the army numbered 7,000, along with several hundred horses. Ground-piercing radar has detected shards still underground that when finally excavated will produce an army in excess of 100,000 soldiers. Sadly the Chinese government has neither the funds nor experienced personnel to finish this task in our lifetime. At the time of my visit, excavation and restoration was crawling along at two days a week with a tiny handful of people on the job, mostly student volunteers working under the tutelage of local university personnel.

Irene and I spend most of a day with the army. Flash photography is not allowed, so I use a tiny tripod. Braced against the railing, I take timed exposures
Soldiers stare at me through the viewfinder, and I think of the history that passed while this army has stood in place. They were assembled before Christ walked the earth, and long after I am gone, they will guard their Emperor. We leave with regrets, for it is not easy to break from its spell.

Near the exit I notice a small man sitting at a table. He is drinking a Coke and smiling at all that pass him. At first I take him for an official greeter, an honored job in such places. Then his image pops into my mind.

I have seen this man in books. It is Mr. Yang Jun Peng, the discoverer of the site that has become China's single largest tourist attraction. More people come to see this army now than visit the Great Wall. Most people walk right by without realizing he has been declared a living national treasure. His job is to sign books and pose for photos, but today, none of his countrymen recognize him.

He is visibly pleased when I approach. We share no common language, but I smile and bow. He puts his arm around me and my wife snaps our photo together. I have given him great face, and a crowd begins to gather. He smiles broadly at the recognition and begins to sign books for his admirers. I slip out the door behind him, and he gives me a final bow.

There is a brilliant sunset outside, and for a moment, I think I hear the commander calling his troops to arms.

MY CHINESE COMMUNIST DINNER

My travel partner Pierre and I had delivered badly needed medical supplies to a remote hospital in northwestern China in exchange for permission to explore areas not usually open to tourists. After making our delivery, Chinese etiquette required our hosts, officials of the Communist party, to thank us properly in the form of a sumptuous banquet.

An official car picked us up at our hotel. We had no idea where we were going as we were taxied through rolling countryside, miles out of town. An hour later we arrived at a military base. There must be some mistake, I thought, as uniformed guards snapped to attention and saluted as we motored past.

One of the cardinal rules of traveling in China is to avoid military bases, especially when carrying cameras, but there I was, a western capitalist, inside a communist military installation with my bag full of what could potentially be perceived as spy tools. Images flashed through my head of being thrown up against a wall and shot for espionage. This was supposed to be a simple thank you dinner. How could this be happening?

I would learn that many of the finest restaurants in northwestern China are reserved for Communist officials. This one, being in the middle of nowhere, just happened to be on an air force base. Fighter jets screeched overhead as we were ushered to meet the military governor of Xinjiang province, our host for the evening, who was surprisingly attired in casual, western style civilian clothing.

"Welcome," he said, sticking out a beefy hand to shake. "You are not writers or spies are you?" And with that he and all his yes men began to chuckle. Pierre and I exchanged a look of bewilderment. I clutched my camera bag in a death grip hoping to absorb it, praying I might be rescued by a stroke or heart attack, when several of the officials' wives emerged with cameras and began to take photos.

This was my reprieve, and I tentatively removed a camera to attempt a few of my own photos. When everyone posed and smiled, my heart began to beat again.

The governor escorted us into the restaurant, a facsimile of a nomadic yurt, designed to soften the militaristic ambiance of the rest of the base.

Inside, we passed buckets of strange creatures that I assumed were about to become our dinner. Live eels writhed in a plastic bucket, and directly inside the door a waiter passed around a tray of fried scorpions as an appetizer. Pinching one between two fingers, the governor put the arthropod to his mouth and took a bite, then gestured for us to eat. They had the texture of Cheetos, tasted like cardboard, and the tiny limbs tickled as they slid down my throat. Then he led us to our table, which held bowls of sunflower seeds.

After being seated, the governors' wife, a stylish lady who spoke excellent English, attached herself to my arm and proceeded to point out the exotic delicacies we would dine on, while loudly spitting sunflower husks onto the floor.

On the platter before me was a mound of baked baby sparrows, curled, fetus-like, and lathered with what appeared to be a chocolate sauce. The sight of the dish caused my fragile traveler's stomach to turn a notch as I pondered how best to approach eating them.

The next dish didn't offer me any reprieve. The governors' wife informed me that it was boiled rabbit embryo, though I never would have guessed it from the writhing mass on the platter: Formless blobs with eyes, it resembled a predigested meal.

Pierre and I exchanged looks, sharing the same thought: Eat or offend our hosts?
I watched the other guests dig in, holding the birds by beak and feet while turning them like miniature corn cobs and crunching tiny bones to suck out the marrow. All around me, little beaks protruded from people's mouths as they sucked brains out of the backs of tiny skulls.

Guests slurped the embryos loudly, like oysters, from a spoon, and I had to remind myself that in China, such noises are a compliment to the chef. I slid one down my throat, fighting the urge to gag. Everyone ate with their hands, smacking their lips and licking their fingers while grimacing from the red-hot sauces. Bodily noises were the order of the evening.

I was already nursing a stomach in revolt at the sight of some of these plates, but to not eat would have insulted my hosts, so I popped a sparrow into my mouth and sucked off the coating, which proved to be a fiery paste made from chili peppers. Fighting back spice-induced tears, I spit the baby bird back into my napkin and looked around – no one had noticed.

Dinner talk was spirited and copious toasts of strong plum wine fueled the evening, so no one was aware I had stopped eating and was only moving my food around with my chopsticks. About halfway through the meal, I felt a tug on my pants and looked under the table to see a kitten sitting on my shoes. Feral cats are quite common throughout China, and this one was sent as my guardian angel.

Moving slowly, I passed my napkin down to the hungry animal. There was a loud crunch as my eager co-conspirator consumed the sparrow, bones and all. The cat appeared ravenous, and I assumed living on a military base where pets are prohibited, this skinny scavenger was more than used to fending for itself. I picked up one of the slippery embryos. It had the con-sistency of a jellyfish and I was careful not to let it slide off my fingers as I bent, as if to eat it, then slipped it to the kitten. Once again, my accomplice consumed everything, licking my fingers for good measure.

I continued to covertly pass it tiny wings, feet, and various other slimy body parts. The kitten did its best to vacuum up food as quickly as I could feed it, and our hosts appeared none the wiser about my secret helper.

Suddenly the cat let out a belch. Not a loud belch, but loud enough for those on either side of me to hear it and I slumped in my chair asking God to swallow me into the earth. With that the Governor stood up and lift-ed his glass to toast me. I did not know at the time that to burp loudly in China is the ultimate compliment to the meal and one's dining companions and since everyone thought I was the culprit, the cat had given me great face by doing so.

As the evening wound down, Pierre and I paid our respects, and in the car on our way back to the city, I had a spirited conversation with the gover-nors' wife about the event. I truly felt I had pulled off a coup, having pho-tographed Communist officials, inside a secure military base, and escaped with my head, all thanks to a homeless animal and I am sure no cat ever made a larger contribution to international relations.

It was only then that I knew I had been made as she leaned close so the driver would not overhear and whispered, "I could not eat much of that stuff either. Would you like to stop and get a burger?"

CRUISING THE YANGTZE

I never wanted to go on a cruise.

The idea of traveling anywhere on one of those giant floating cities was just anathema to my way of traveling. However, when my wife and I first went to China we were offered a local deal I could not turn down.

We would go down the Yangtze River from ChunChing to Shanghai, through the three Gorges that were about to be lost forever when the giant dam project at Wuhan would raise the current water lever almost three hundred feet. It was a final chance to see one of Chinas' great natural wonders before it disappeared forever. We were offered passage on an aging wooden Chinese cruise boat that had nothing in common with the modern giants that filled our home harbor. It was small and simple, close to the water and not ten stories high like its modern cousins.

I found its plainness appealing with simple cabins, a spacious dining room, and large open decks for viewing the scenery. Best of all, I was told the passengers would be local Chinese. When I balked at the tiny beds, an upgrade to a suite quickly sealed the deal for us.

My wife and I were the only non-Chinese waiting on the dock, yet everyone was unfailingly polite to us. People bowed as we caught them staring at us strange looking westerners and whispered comments filtered through the crowd. Once the gangplank was lowered there was a mass scramble to board with so much pushing and shoving that we stood aside, just watching with open mouthed amazement.

Even though we boarded last, we were swept along by a human tide as people bowled each over getting to their cabins as though they would be taken from them. There was much pushing and shoving, and inside our cabin we left our door open to combat the humidity and found ourselves the central attraction for a sea of curious faces. People just stopped in our doorway and stared openly at us.

We were anxious to mingle with the people as we headed for the dining room on day one. It was already crowded when we arrived but you could have heard a pin drop when we walked in. All eyes turned to us, and everyone froze. Smiling to all, we took an unoccupied seat and this sent an audible gasp through the crowd. We had unwittingly committed our first cultural faux-paux, sitting among the local people. A red-faced waiter quickly ushered us to a corner table under a sign that read "Foreigner seating." With us in our proper place, the room suddenly became animated again.

I noticed all the tables of seated Chinese held only chopsticks while our table had knives, forks and spoons. My wife and I often eat with chopsticks and asked for them. This caused a general buzz throughout the dining crowd as people craned their necks and commented about the round eyes who had mastered this ancient form of eating. We vainly hoped that perhaps this was enough to cancel our seating mistake.

Rather than be offended by our segregation, we chalked it up to being in one of the most class-conscious societies on earth. We were foreigners here and like it or not, we would remain outsiders. This was a chance for us to observe from the sidelines.

The food was served buffet style and we watched incredulously as our dinner companions pushed and shoved their way to the heaping platters. Even the children seemed to have no manners as they scrambled to fill their plates. There was more than enough food, but people were grabbing it and piling their plates like starving prisoners. We waited for a lull in the frenzy before getting our food then sat to watch in amazement as people gobbled things up before going back for more. It seemed impossible for anyone to eat the amounts they were heaping onto their plates. Noisy eating in China is a sign to the chef that the food is good, but these folks were over the top for the quality of this ships' cuisine. Loud and obnoxious bodily sounds filled the room along with the accompanying aromas and there was more belching and lip smacking than I had ever heard.

The more people ate, the louder the crescendo of their voices grew until we gave up trying to talk to each other. These people were seized by a feeding frenzy.

Before leaving, most people filled plates with deserts and retired to their cabins with several pieces of pie and cake.

After dinner I asked a crewman, a Mormon missionary from Utah, about what we had witnessed. He told me these people were from the provinces and had saved for years to take a cruise like this. For many, coming to this port had been their first time in a city.

Standing in line was an unknown concept for them, and as for the food, while nothing fancy, for them it was a dream coming true. Most of them had never seen so much food, and for probably the only time in their lives, they could eat all they wanted. It was not a cultural matter. It was a poverty matter. Chinese peasants are the bottom of the national food chain. These people were being offered unlimited gluttony for the first time ever. It took me back to my days in the Army where the rule was "Take all you want, but eat all you take."

Now that I understood, I returned to my cabin determined to join the crowd at the next meal.

In the morning we made our way to breakfast, pushing and shoving with the best of them. My wife threw a couple of elbows while reaching for the egg rolls and I got in a couple good shots over the bird drop soup. I even added a nice little body block to an aging Ama who was particularly belligerent until I hip checked her.

We seemed to gain a little face this time as we sat at the "Foreigner table." I even noticed a few of our fellow passengers giving a slight bow in our direction. Our attempts to fit in were being acknowledged. At lunch I used my superior size to keep moving forward, then piled my plate high to approving nods all around. This hit a chord with some folks who stepped aside for me with a polite laugh. We were getting the hang of things.

Between meals we made daily excursions with these people. We boarded San Pans one day for a leisurely paddle up a river about to be flooded by the new dam project. We were offered the front seat for this trip and were asked to take pictures of several of our group. At the ancient city of Fung Du, we were the first to be ushered into the temples.

By the end of day three we were being asked to pose for everyone's camera and I found myself standing arm in arm with smiling faces like some minor celebrity.

At breakfast the next day a portly gentleman came up and gave me a good shove. Before I could react I saw his smile and realized he was having some fun with me. It had taken very little input from us to fit in. We were still expected to eat at the "Foreigners" table but having proven we were willing to fight for our meal, were now officially part of the group.

At one dinner a tiny lady I had not seen before was unusually adept at cutting in front of people and maneuvering to the best dishes. When she came at me she literally gave me a body block, bouncing off my occidental girth in the process. Undaunted, she came right back and tried to elbow me aside from the Mu Shu Pork. Now it truly was a matter of face and I sidestepped her next onslaught and gave her a shove from behind.

She hit the floor, howling as though I had knifed her. Everyone turned to the scene for a moment, looking at her then back to me. Thinking I may have overdone it this time, I quickly relaxed as conversation returned to normal with people stepping over the tiny lady on their way to more broccoli beef. Apparently what I had done was well within the boundary of proper meal-time etiquette. In this part of China at least, it was street dog fighting.

The following day I saw the same lady elbowing her way to the front of the line but when she saw me, she stepped to another table flashing me her best scowl.

Pulling into the smog of Shanghai I was saddened to leave our intrepid travelers. We were about to re-enter a world where standing in line was a way of life. It suddenly seemed very dull to me. I had come to enjoy being the brunt of inside jokes and to watch that evolve into a full-blown mutual respect. I have always thought travel to be the great educator and this trip had enlightened me no end.

To this day in China, many minorities are not recognized by the government and have no official status as citizens. At least on this boat, these people were treated, if only for a brief time, to life as it should be. Now most of them would return to dirt poor farms and villages with a memory and stories to last a lifetime.

We stood on the dock staring at the enormous pile of luggage heaped before us. It had been dumped en mass in the center of the dock and finding one's bag required the same skills we had just mastered in the dining room. When all bags had been claimed, ours were nowhere to be seen. A crewman seeing our distress asked us to follow him and there in a corner were our duffle bags under a sign that read, "Foreigner baggage."

Before jumping into a cab that was beyond the financial means of our fellow travelers, we were asked to pose for one final photo. After shaking hands, with much bowing all around, the cab door was opened and we were shoved inside by several smiling faces.

Pulling away I looked out the back window and saw two couples fighting over a rickshaw.

ONE MINE AT A TIME

Stepping into a live mine field gives one a whole new appreciation for the term, concentration.

Akira tells me to follow him closely and I am practically in his back pocket.

The sun is a swirling ball that would be at home in a Van Gogh painting, frying my brains under my helmet and visor that is so close to my nose I feel I am suffocating. I stop every few feet to raise it for a quick breath and quickly lower it to escape Akiras' wrath for disobeying an order. Under my frontal body armor sweat pours as if I were a saturated sponge. The post monsoon humidity in the Cambodian jungle is bad enough without 20 pounds of body armor and three cameras. Having to wear all of this is ironic because if I were to step on a mine it would be useless.

Much of the field has been burned away, cleared of brush, while the square areas yet to be checked are outlined with red twine anchored at each corner with a bright red deaths head that screams, "Mines" That eyeless skull is everywhere, a constant reminder that this country has known war for most of its existence. The Khmer Rouge leader, Pol Pot, called land mines, "The perfect soldier" as they were designed to maim rather than kill.

Being chosen as a CNN HERO in 2010 brought Akira international fame, and in 2012 he won the Manhae Peace Prize awarded by South Korea, but those awards changed nothing for him. This man who now meets with prime ministers and billionaires is humble and self-effacing, the kind of guy who gets lost in a crowd were it not for the fact that he is a living national treasure. For him there is only the work.

Akira is only truly happy in the jungle, working, sleeping in a hammock, trapping snakes and birds for food, and sharing his teams' danger. Orphaned by age 8, an approximation since there are no written records; Akira was taken in by the Khmer Rouge and made a child soldier, trained as an explosives expert, and made to plant land mines; a job he admits to becoming quickly adept at. At 13 he was captured and forced to join the invading Vietnamese army, fighting against his former friends, while still planting mines. According to him, he could easily lay 100 in a single day. At 14, when the Vietnamese withdrew from Cambodia, he was drafted into the Cambodian army and made an officer, one of the most skilled demolition experts in Cambodia while still almost a child and a combat veteran of three separate armies. At 19 he was recruited by the United Nations but his growing awareness of what he had done as a child brought him an epiphany. He would not work for anyone else again. Instead, he would devote the rest of his life to removing the deadly objects he himself had installed. Eventually he founded the Cambodia Self Help De-mining NGO.

When a mine is found a small square of reclaimed TNT with a radio controlled detonator is laid next to it, Akira orders everyone to back off a paced 75 yards and to kneel down for the explosion. Even from that distance, the detonation of a small antipersonnel mine is like a whack in the chest from a hammer. There is a physical shock wave that invades your body. I watch a mushroom cloud of dirt rise 40 feet in the air as one more mine is eliminated.

Kneeling behind one of the de-miners, a young girl in her 20's, I synch my breathing to hers, moving as she moves, sliding my knees ever so gently, watching for any tell-tale sign or a depression in the dirt. She uses gardening shears to clear overhanging brush and runs a knife around the edges of her detector to make sure it is functioning properly before passing it almost unperceptively over the ground from left to right then back again several times, lightly as a butterfly. It is like watching paint dry and yet the only sound is the beating of my own heart.

 It is the most intense feeling, senses heightened, sound magnified, ears scanning for the slightest nuance, eyes probing through the dirt itself. When that six inch swath gives no warning she moves the red painted board forward to the limit of her scan, another few inches made safe. In an hour we move only a few feet when a screech comes over the headphones and she kneels, slowly begins to clear dirt, inserting her trowel at an angle so as not to apply any pressure on the mine should that prove to be the culprit. A mere 10 pounds of pressure is all it takes to enter the hereafter. With infinite patience she scoops dirt away revealing the green curved rim of a Russian made anti-personnel mine.

Word goes out over the radio and Akira comes running. While we wait for him I am told this young lady is the mother of three and I try to imagine what I would feel if my own mother removed landmines for a living. Akira calls me over to see this mine before blowing it. Akira laughs at my trembling hand, only inches away from a device that can send me to my next life in the blink of an eye. A few minutes later as another blast rocks the jungle he has lived up to his slogan, "One mine at a time."

This team has chosen a life of self-denial that is almost as monastic as the saffron robed monks their country is known for. In their military fatigues bearing the logo of the de-mining organization, they are treated as local heroes wherever they go and Akira is rapidly attaining superstar status. By his own estimate, it will take another decade to rid Cambodia of most of its land mines.

When I leave I take a final look at Akira sitting by a campfire laughing with his troops. It had been a good day. He had blown up three mines.

A LIGHT IN THE DARKNESS

This is a story for people of faith.

Years ago in a cave, in a ruin, in a Cambodian jungle, I spent less than an hour with a female hermit who to this day has impacted my life.

I have always considered my travels to be a learning process and have sought out those who might advance me slightly on the correct religious path, taking bits and pieces from each belief and forging them into my own.

On my first trip to Cambodia I spent much of my time deep in the jungles with Buddhist monks who welcomed me as a seeker. It was there that I learned most Cambodian men spend time as a novice monk before deciding to take vows or return to the secular life, and that one out of six remained with the brotherhood.
I had always seen women at the monasteries and ignorantly assumed them to be housekeepers or servants and only learned they were nuns through a very unique event.

Almost one year later a local guide was driving me through the jungle to a distant temple when we were stopped by one of the numerous freelance soldiers left over from Khmer Rouge days who make their living shaking down people like me who venture a little too far off the beaten path. I had just handed him some money when a tiny woman appeared, it seemed, from out of nowhere. She barely came up to my shoulder and was the color of beetlenut with a shaved head, wore a white blouse, black drawstring pants, and was barefoot. Her milky eye was sightless and her grin was missing a few teeth but this did not stop her from thrusting her alms bowl between the startled soldier and me.

We were both taken off guard by her silent appearance I and fumbled for a couple bills that I dropped into her bowl while the soldier was apparently so ashamed of being caught in his actions towards me, that he gave her part of the bribe I had just paid him. The woman turned and without saying a word, disappeared into the jungle. As the soldier waved me on he spat in her direction and said "Yiyay Chi" which I later found out was Khmer for nun. She was the first one I met.

The jungles of Cambodia are filled with ornate shrines, massive stone edifices with a larger than life carved Buddha, colorful prayer flags, incense burners and candles, all in danger of being reclaimed by the jungle. Each is manned by a praetorian guard of chattering monkeys, spitting cobras, saffron robed monks, and nuns. They dot the remote countryside in the most unlikely places; small islands of beauty in a land devastated by 2,000 years of war and monuments to the indestructability of the human spirit.

At first sight, these shrines are so overwhelming you must ask how did they get there, and then quickly realize the massive amount of labor and cost necessary not just to build them in such a place but also to maintain them in a hostile environment where vines can crush a stone monument in a few months. The money is minimal, coming from the trickle of visitors bold enough to venture this deep into the jungle, and the rest is done with sweat, love, and faith.

I spent long hours in conversation with the monks at these temples, talking well into the night of all things both spiritual and temporal and always came away in awe of these simple jungle dwellers, most of whom had no formal education and yet were so fervent in their beliefs and happy in their lives as to make me question my own sense of purpose. I also noticed that during these times the nuns would fade into the background, sweeping, tending to candles or incense, always busy but with downcast eyes, and never looking in my direction. I was told that most of them were either poor or widows, and lacking the means to remain in the material world, had entered the spiritual one to build karma in their final years for the life that was to follow. I came to believe they might outnumber the monks, but were simply overshadowed by the colorful robes and more outgoing personalities.

I began to seek them out, this unknown quantity, intentionally making eye contact and eventually gaining a slight smile from more than one, but whenever I tried to begin a conversation they would usually put a finger to their mouth and signal me to silence. I took this to mean their commitment to another place was total and they had no time to give to outside visitors.

On more than one occasion I was surprised to find monks in civilian clothes, smoking cigarettes or drinking coffee, obviously seeing no contradiction in this change of lifestyle, and eventually met a few who enjoyed local celebrity status, reducing their position to a job rather than a calling. But the nuns seemed to me to be more singly focused, going about their work with quiet efficiency and subtle, almost imperceptible smiles, as though they were privy to a great secret. As a whole, I have never met more humble people.

While crossing the country I had avoided going to Angkor, knowing it to be an anthill of tourists, surpassing even the Great Wall of China in popularity, but finally entered the complex early one morning and made my way to Prasat Bayan, the center of Angkor Thom, former capitol of the Khmer ruler, Jayavarman V11 the Mahayana Buddhist king, and famous for its 216 gigantic carved stone faces.

My only purpose was to visit these monuments before the sea of people arrived and I was wandering alone through one of mankind's' great artistic achievements, marveling at the craftsmanship that produced these monuments so long ago without modern technology and musing about how one small section of just one face could be the life work of a single person. The Khmer carved stone like most people breathe and they did breathe life into their work. The entire history of the Khmer civilization is preserved in stone at the Angkor complex, a gigantic granite book for the world to read. Walking through Angkor Thom, giant stone eyes watch your every move.

Some scholars believe the stone faces of Angkor Thom are those of Jayavarman himself, watching over his realm throughout history, while others claim them to be representations of Lokesvara, the bodhisattva of compassion, but either way, this holy place of worship has attracted pilgrims for centuries.

I saw a small girl climbing the side of a temple face with a shawl full of fruit under her arm, and just before nearing the top, she disappeared. I waited and watched to see the girl emerge from somewhere on the rock face hidden to me from below and when she reached the ground I asked what she was doing. She just pointed up and said, "The lady."

Those two words intrigued me enough that I began to make my way up the great stone face, finding small makeshift altars along the way where people had left behind burned candles, offerings of food, and even a photo of what I assumed was a deceased relative. Suddenly, just above me, a friendly face peered over the edge.

She had short white hair and an enigmatic Mona Lisa smile. Her face was a roadmap of hard times and yet her age was indecipherable. She radiated peace.

Cresting the ledge I found her seated on a stone slab in a smoke filled cell that most likely had been occupied for prayer and meditation for centuries. There was no furniture or bed, nor was there room for any. She was clothed all in white with a shawl over her shoulder; spotless in her closet like cell, and as our eyes met I had an overwhelming sense of being in the presence of more than just an ordinary nun.

I had met holy hermits before, in Greece, Africa, and China, some self-proclaimed, while others truly gave off an aura of sanctity, but all of them had been men and few had impressed me.

When I entered her cell, this lady patted the stone, and as I sat next to her she covered my hand with her own in the most natural manner and I felt an energy enter my body I had not known before, truly feeling I was in communion with a living saint.

I studied her for a moment; eyes closed, already in another place, but compassionate enough to share it with me. Had I not seen the little girl I never would have found this woman, or would I? I believe important events happen for a reason and perhaps the afternoon would have found another way to bring the two of us together. Maybe her soul needed to touch mine for her own reasons.

We sat in silence for an undetermined time as I was lost in my own serenity and when she finally lifted her hand from mine, I knew instinctively it was time to leave. We had not spoken as there was no need. I had received more from this woman in those few minutes than I had gained in a lifetime of wandering, and if the reader needs more explanation than that then I am not a gifted enough writer to impart it in words.

As I got up to leave I was stunned by the panorama spread before me, towering temples, lush green jungle encased by rolling red hills, and all of it enveloped by a shimmering yellow mist cast by the afternoon sun. I swear the color of that moment was more intense than any I had seen before.

Such a view could not help but elevate the spirit of any person and I felt closer to God in that moment than I had in a very long time.

I probably could have jumped to the ground just then but when I looked up at the black stone face towering over me there was no evidence of human habitat, let alone an enlightened one. Everything was normal once again and yet I was different inside.

As I said before, this is a story of faith. Perhaps what I experienced was only what Buddhists call "Maya" or illusion, or maybe it was simply my own subconscious needing such an moment that I willed myself to believe in it. I will take either version, because it worked for me.

While I have no illusions of ever attaining her degree of spiritual enlightenment, there have been many troubled times in my life when this woman has returned to my thoughts at a needed moment and I know it was by design.

Perhaps there really are guardian angels but I doubt that I will know for sure in this lifetime; but if there are, I met mine in a cave cell in Cambodia.

GIVING FACE IN CHINA

Pierre and I watched the old man for about an hour, meticulously carving his spoons while seemingly invisible to the sea of people passing him by.

He was weathered and bent with a long gray beard, sitting in a heap on a dirty blanket, legs folded under him, sheathed in knee high boots with ragged peasant pants tucked inside. He wore a striped jacket reminiscent of a death camp survivor, one of millions of faceless street people who somehow manage to get through each day in a police state that shows no mercy.

His four cornered hat and beard identified him as a Uyghur, an Eastern European Muslim who are the majority in western China but looked down on by their class conscious rulers, the Han. While officially Chinese they could not be more culturally different, victims of ever changing lines on governments maps. Uyghurs have occupied western China for centuries but will never be Chinese. They had been in open revolt over their treatment for several weeks prior to our arrival, bombing numerous police stations, demanding the autonomy the Chinese government has granted them on paper but never gave in reality, and that is what we had come to document. The old man was beyond fighting age but never too old to be a victim of prejudice.

We watched from a distance as people passed his blanket, some kicking his spoons away while others stepped on them. China has always been cruel to its people and indifferent to its poor, but being born a Uyghur is the bottom of the heap. One teenage punk grabbed a spoon and ran before the old man knew what was happening, but this was his life and you do not reach old age in this land without accepting abuse.

Pierre and I were both old China hands, used to being charged foreigner prices and having guns stuck in our faces, as that is the cost of solo travel in a culture that feeds on paranoia. I could identify with the old man.

It was our last day in Kashgar and just for the hell of it Pierre and I had wandered to the public square in front of the big yellow mosque. It had been ten years since Pierre had met the old man on the same corner, whittling wooden spoons for a few pennies, obviously making enough to survive but never prosper, which is in itself an accomplishment for the lower masses of China.

Pierre has a nose for such nuances of humanity, ferreting out the unsung street people and getting them to share epic tales that most travelers simply pass by without noticing. So neither of us was surprised to see the old man sitting there now, a little grayer, a little more bent than remembered, but he still held his ancient pen knife and a pile of hand carved wooden spoons still shared his blanket on the street curb. We watched him from a bench while Pierre told me of that meeting so long ago when he had bought one of the old man's spoons, paying ten times his asking price because that is what Pierre does for those less fortunate.

Pierre had brought me one of those spoons, intricate, delicate, a utensil so finely wrought that it should never be used; only admired. The old man was an artist. Had he been born anywhere else he would probably have an atelier and clients, but in China, he was issued from the wrong womb and trapped within his cultural group.

Pierre thought the old man to be over 90 at that first meeting which would make him a centurion now and I wondered how many of those years he had been a wood carver.

Both Pierre's and my home are filled with the detritus of years of remote travel and I wanted my own artifact from this spoon carver. I wanted to shake his hand and tell him I travel to seek stories about people like him, stories from the collective memory of mankind that enlighten all of us, and I wanted a piece of this man's life for my shelf at home that holds so many other stories brought back from the corners of this earth. But neither of us spoke Chinese so the words went unsaid. What we could do though was give the man face.

We walked over and squatted in front of him noticing that one opaque eye no longer took in the world around him, but then again, his spoons showed such workmanship that I think perhaps this artist limited his vision to his immediate surroundings long ago. He looked up warily at our approach, while his gnarled hands continued to work the wood with the assurance of a master sculptor.

Kashgar is still far off the beaten tourist path so two tall occidentals kneeling on what appeared to be a beggars blanket in the town square immediately attracted attention. The curious began to gather as Pierre reached into his jacket and produced the spoon he had bought from the old man a decade ago. As he handed it to him those sensitive fingers immediately began to caress the surface and a toothless smile spread across the ancient face. A work of art had returned to its master and he knew we were friends, reaching out a hand to both of us.

By this time a significant crowd had gathered and in China a crowd also brings the police. The two officers were visibly surprised to see Pierre and I at the center of this gathering and I have no doubt they would have been cruel to the old man had we round eyes not been there. Nothing rattles the beaurocratic goons of the Chinese hinterlands like the presence of an outsider. If you stand up to their ingrained bullying tactics they usually back down, often making fools of themselves. They simply do not know how to act around foreigners, terrified of the truth we may carry back to the outside world. Knowing this, we were ready to strike a blow for the little man.

Pierre and I each picked up a spoon, making a great display of admiring them. With people pushing and shoving to get close to this strange performance we made a point of pulling out a large roll of bills. With all eyes on him, Pierre began to count out money, slowly so all could see. As the count grew an audible murmur spread through the crowd. At about $20 U.S. Pierre handed it to the old man, a fair price to us but a veritable fortune in rural China, especially for a simple wooden spoon. We heard the incredulous comments needing no interpreter. "How could these foreigners give so much money to this old Uyghur?"

With that we both stood up, bowed to him deeply, and turned to walk away, leaving two gaping policemen and a stunned crowd of people on the corner. It was a simple act, but in Kashgar it was open defiance against the status quo that only a foreigner could get away with. The old man was smiling from ear to ear.

We retreated across the street, into a store where no one could see us to watch what came next. The police who normally would have routed the old man with their batons were ordering people to walk around him, and everyone began to give him a wide berth. They were no longer trampling on his wares and in fact a few of them dropped money onto his blanket without taking any spoons. The Han are such programmed automatons that they would now show the old man respect, whether they felt it or not, understood why or not, simply because their masters had ordered it. Our simple act had given the man great face and that crosses all barriers in the paradox that is China.

Kashgar is a place of routines, where people go through the motions of life each day without really living because there are no other options. When Thoreau wrote, "The mass of men lead lives of quiet desperation" he could have been speaking of modern day China. I am sure the story of two strange Americans honoring an old Uyghur spread quickly, changing with each telling while the facts recede into myth.

Today the old man's photo sits on my den shelf with several of his spoons, and that day is a story I relive over and over.

TALES FROM AFRICA

REJUVENATION

I step ashore onto the sandy beach and hand the boatman a full day's wages hoping he will return at the agreed time to pick me up.

His toothy smile tells me he will, and at worst, I will share a hut tonight with a pig or cow.

The island, in the middle of the Niger River in Mali, is a shimmering mass of brown leather because the boatman has left me in the center of the Fulani cattle herd. The sun dances off polished horns while an overpowering aroma of dung washes over me on a light breeze. The Fulani, indigenous nomads of West Africa, are traditional cattle herders and, I am told, pretty good hands with a knife.

I have long sought out such cultures in places where my body, mind, and soul are, without realizing it, weary from human artificiality. I seek them out not only to learn, but to find solitude, where the whisper of a breeze is a symphony and the flap of a butterfly's wing is almost a prayer.

My early travels were to the usual tourist destinations that while fun, ultimately left me disappointed, realizing they were only variations of where I had come from. I had to acknowledge a deep seated need to read more pages of the book, to wander where others had not yet been. I have never been one to relax on a vacation. For me, travel is a way to learn and experience. Ultimately I was drawn to leave the beaten path in search of truly different ways of life. I did not realize at the time that I had begun a quest that would ultimately lead me to ponder my own place in the grand cosmic scheme.

It was only after my first encounters with remote tribal cultures that I realized the deep inbred connection these people, whom most of us in the west would refer to as "primitive," have to the land, its fellow creatures, and ultimately to their idea of a deity; all connections that I had as a child but had at least partially surrendered without my knowledge, over a period of many years, due to an unwitting immersion in the material world. Where I once considered such people to be simple in a derogatory way, I now saw them to be that in an enlightened way. A way that I believe at one time was possessed by all humankind before it was watered down.

While the march of technology and progress is inevitable, and for the most part a good thing, it is a by-product of the human condition that results from our insatiable quest for knowledge, and it does have a dark side; that being the gradual removal from our origins and the replacement of the natural world with a manufactured one.

Living in bustling metropolises, being bombarded with electronic media around the clock and spending most waking hours staring at electronic screens or talking to them has dulled the senses that early man once possessed to a remarkable degree, and with that has come the slow degradation of our natural appreciation for nature. Because of this I periodically flee from my own kind.

No sooner do I enter a milieu like that of the Fulani than my biological clock slows, my heart rate drops, and I shift to a pace that does not require a watch. Suddenly the absence of mechanical sound is music, and my vestigial senses, stored away in my modern home, begin to awaken. Colors assume an unknown vibrancy while tastes and smells expand to a new importance; the song of a bird becomes an aria and the jump of a fish is a ballet.

None of this is meant as an indictment of the modern world. I live in that world and make my living there, enjoying it as much as anyone, but I also realize the need for balance, and that for a life to have substantial meaning there must be equal parts of the old and new. I am of the modern world but seek knowledge of its origins in the old one. How would things be different if I were the Fulani? What would I think of this strange looking visitor who is nothing like I have ever seen, showing up like a nomad and wearing so many clothes?

As I walk among the baying cattle I cannot help but wonder what is in a cow's mind? Such a thought, I know, would never come to me in the city, but here, under God's cerulean sky, I ponder whether these animals might not be great personages in the universe they inhabit, thinking that just because I cannot communicate with them I am not necessarily on a higher plane. Perhaps what I perceive as their blank, fish like stares, are in fact an insightful summing up of a bizarre looking intruder, or maybe they are deliberately ignoring me, being unworthy of their notice. In their world, the cow I just pushed aside might be a Nobel Prize winner for study in human husbandry.

I stop to watch a man milking and he playfully squirts a spray in my direction, offering me at once a welcome and a safe passage to his realm. As my mind begins to awaken to its new surroundings I am taking mental notes faster than I can process them. A cascade of images, thoughts, and ideas, has been presented to me in this vast open arena of life. The crunch of my feet on cattle fodder becomes a crescendo and the baying of five thousand bovine voices wash over me like a mantra.

Children materialize, sprites on the wind, and in a moment I have two connected to the fingers on both hands telling me I am currently the most interesting diversion in their life while knowing I might be replaced by an animal at any second. We walk along with them yelling excitedly, in what I assume is announcement of my arrival, and it occurs to me that this simple act of touch, so full of humanity here, would most likely be misinterpreted in my home town. I spend the whole day with these people, the women with sometimes bared breasts, the men tall and hard like polished ebony. We have no common language but none is needed. Smiles, gestures, and laughter, require no translation. I am welcome here.

A white haired elder whose age I would guess at between fifty and one hundred, sends a toothless smile at me from the doorway of his hut where he is weaving straw thatch and his assumed wife waves shyly, looking every inch like an elf. There is no waste here and no graffiti. It is void of all modern trappings and the people live in the moment. Everyone nods and offers a welcome and I know this is the kind of day a traveler prays for.

These are nomads, those who wander as a way of life. Their lack of a permanent home insulates them from the electronic world, where as if they had one, they would at some point most likely be exposed and perhaps seduced by it, but living as they do, they are pure and untouched, an organic part of the whole. The Fulani claim the fringes of the great Sahel as their home, wandering wherever there is water and feed for their cattle, living in grass huts woven on the spot, used for a couple weeks and then abandoned. They move with and like the wind, free and unencumbered, a striking contrast to my own object strewn life.

I remember reading long ago the works of Bruce Chatwin who wrote at length about nomads and who considered walking to be a form of meditation. According to Chatwin, the simple act of walking could cure most physical maladies. Chatwin believed walking to be the natural state of Homo Sapiens who ambulated as a way of life long before the invention of the wheel.

I have always been a great walker so if Mr. Chatwin is correct, then perhaps I have some deeply implanted homing device that motivates me to walk out the door and keep on going until I have enough stories to come home and share them with the world; a primordial GPS, built into my species long before the last ice age as my forbearers crossed the Bering land bridge to settle what would eventually become Rodeo Drive. I am simply one of the rare ones that did not get the memo that we no longer wander but live in massive villages.

The children lead me on for a half mile, past their herds to the southern tip of the island where white, fresh water pelicans are lunge feeding, diving like kamikazes, headlong into the waters churning with catfish. Many just float on the surface scooping up fish in their basket like pouches. A red and green humming bird shimmers in the sunlight like flying jewelry and I feel light, unencumbered and part of the scene. We follow the shoreline back, the children skipping stones over the water, while I imagine my life if I had been born one of them.

If such were the case I could make fire in a rainstorm and find a good meal under a rock, but I would know nothing of television, telephones or the internet. I would probably be closer to my Creator than I am now but being a work in progress I am always headed in that direction, and this day has taken me a few steps further along the path. I certainly would not voluntarily trade places with any of them but at the same time know instinctively that none of them would want my life either. One way is not better than the other, only different.

As the shadows begin to grow long I acknowledge this to be one fine day. The Fulani have jump started my batteries, recharged a life grown soft from a leather sofa in front of a television, and while I cannot wait to return to that sofa and my soul mate who waits there, I am grateful once again that the old world has rejuvenated the new.

I walk to the waiting boat stepping over dozens of tiny sand crabs, while the pelicans that are as common as flies here sit just offshore in hopes of begging an easy meal from the fisherman. I turn to wave goodbye to all the children and one rushes forward, pressing a tiny object into my hand. Our eyes meet and I think this tyke is going to amount to something one day. He runs bowlegged and naked to join his companions while I rub my fingers over his present to feel it before looking.

It is a small hand modeled statue of a hump backed bull, kneaded from river mud and slow baked in the broiling sun but still pliable, a piece sculpted from a young mans' soul. It is a miniature version of the bulls whose intelligence I pondered, and was made, I believe, especially for me.

It is at once a gift, a work of art, and will become a reminder that we are all the same under our colors, but sometimes you just have to listen to the silence in order to know that.

PAST TIMBUKTU

There are places whose names carry an instant association with the romantic and exotic, and for me the foremost has always been Timbuktu.

I am not sure when I first heard the name, but recall as a child that nothing could be "As far away as Timbuktu." Until the turn of the 19th century, many people in the western world considered it a fable much like Shangri La or Atlantis.

For years it had been my siren call, but it would not be enough to just go there. I wanted to experience it through local eyes, and if possible to stay among the Berber nomads for whom Timbuktu is their southern base, but could I, a white Christian, enter such a private Muslim enclave, and if so, what would be the consequences?

My entre to this world was a Tuareg aristocrat by the name of Halis Al Moctar, who made his living running a local tour operation out of a cyber café, taking tourists into the desert by camel for day trips. When I told him of my desire to travel with Tuaregs he was overjoyed. Apparently I was the first interloper who wanted to "go" Tuareg. He assured me my ethnicity and religious beliefs would pose no obstacles and even provided me with his own robes and tagelmoust (Headgear).

Timbuktu was founded in the 11th century by Tuareg nomads as a camp by the Niger River in Mali, West Africa, at the southern tip of the Sahara Desert, and quickly established itself as a rest stop for both north and south traveling camel caravans. The first written references to the Tuaregs came from the Greek Historian Herodotus, around 450 B.C. who believed them to have originated in either Egypt or Libya many centuries before Christ. He referred to them as Canaanites which translates roughly into "Purple people."

They are a Berber ethnic group whose numbers today approach one million and they are widely spread throughout Niger, Mali, Algeria, Burkina Faso and Libya, with smaller numbers in Morocco. They are traditional nomads, who owe allegiance to no particular country, and consider the Sahara to be their true home. They have a different name for this desert in each of the countries it occupies, and consider it to be many separate deserts. Sahara is a term known only in the west.

For over two thousand years they have hauled gold, salt, and slaves across North Africa to the great port cities such as Mopti and Dakar. The term, "Tuareg" is derived from the area in their assumed ancestral home in Libya called Fezzan Targa, combined with a misinterpretation of the Arabic root TRQ, having a quiloquial meaning of "Abandoned by God," a term they have applied to themselves after losing most of their traditional desert homelands over the centuries by foreign conquest and the political intrigues of their own local governments. They refer to themselves most commonly as Kel Tamasheq or "Those who speak Tamasheq" their native tongue, and also Kel Tagelmoust, or "Wearers of the veil." In Mali, the majority also speak Arabic and French.

Timbuktu has been the southern terminus of their range and was both a meeting and resting place for their caravans since before recorded history. It is surrounded by open desert, and when sandstorms blow, which is a daily occurrence; it can be inaccessible for days. By the mid-13th century it was part of the Mali Empire, ruled by Muslims, and the hub of a thriving economic conglomerate.

By the 15th century the Songhai Empire had taken over and began to build great mosques and universities, turning Timbuktu into a scholar's haven for Islamic learning. Its libraries were equal to the famed depositories at Alexandria, Egypt. During the rule of the Songhai, Timbuktu was the epitome of culture and sophistication. To its inhabitants, it was the center of the world.

This golden age lasted until the 16th century when Morocco invaded and ended the Songhai rule. At the same time Portugal commanded the seas and began establishing trade with the port cities all along the west coast of Africa, effectively negating the importance of the camel caravans. It was far quicker to sail goods to ports than to haul them for weeks on end through the desert. This combination began a gradual decline of the city that has continued to this day.

Now there are countless stories about the origin of the name Timbuktu.

In the Tamasheq language, tin means both place and well. Buktu was the name of a real woman who lived at the oasis before it bore her name. The Tuaregs, going into the desert, had no wish to part with their valuables at a bandit's gunpoint along the trail, and it soon became known that Buktu was a person of trust with whom one could leave their belongings. From there it is a logical leap to the name Timbuktu meaning, the well or place of the lady Buktu. The "o" was added later as one of a half dozen different spellings, depending on who you are talking to at the moment. This is the most common of many stories, and at the Timbuktu Museum today, there is a well in the courtyard that is supposed to be Buktus' original well, but after all this time, who can really know?

A different and less romantic version of the names origin comes from scholars who claim Buktu is a local Songhai word meaning "Woman with a big navel" while a less kindly interpretation means "Woman with a big lump" And yet a third variation says it simply means a depression between sand dunes, which is what Timbuktu actually is. The reader can choose.

By the turn of the 18th century, Western Europe had begun to hear stories of this place but mostly thought it to be a fable, which would have been news to the Tuaregs if they had known of the existence of western Europe. So, in 1788 a group of upper class English officers, probably in their cups late at night in a pub, established the "Association for the Discovery of Interior Portions of Africa." They commissioned a colorful, and inebriated Scottish surgeon named Mungo Park, a self- styled adventurer, to lead an expedition to determine if Timbuktu actually existed, and to fix its' location on a map. Once he hit the road, he was probably sorry he ever started drinking with those chaps.

His expedition was plagued by disaster, most of his party was killed by bandits, and he never reached the city. On his second attempt to penetrate the mysteries of central Africa he drowned in a river.

In 1806 a French explorer with more guts than experience named Rene Callie claimed to have reached Timbuktu as part of the original offer that now included significant prize money to anyone proving its' existence. He returned home via a camel caravan through Morocco and arrived back in Paris to great acclaim, but when he could not produce physical proof of his visit, he was discounted by the local press and entered history as a fraudulent and defeated man.

In 1826, a Scotsman named Gordon Laing, a Major in the British army, left his new bride of two days to pursue the trail to fame and fortune. We know he achieved his goal as several letters from the city actually reached his wife and told of the hostility of the Tuaregs towards him, thinking his presence signaled an onslaught of Europeans. Laing was lured into the desert after 38 days in Timbuktu, where he was ambushed and killed by the Tuaregs, or so the story goes.

In 1990 Timbuktu was added to the UNESCO (the United Nations Economic, Scientific and Cultural Organization) list of World Heritage Sites, and declared "in danger" from the harsh environment, and as such it receives some funding for its restoration and conservation. Cursed by an ever shrinking population, Timbuktu continues to cling to life, refusing to die.

It is a low, brown city, mostly hidden under a layer of sand. But that is a disservice to the color brown. It is a brown filtered through blowing sand and baked by a relentless sun. It is a brown full of mountain purple and sunset yellow. If you stare at the city for a while, it will cover half the color spectrum but in the end you will say, it is brown. There are neither tall buildings nor anything that remotely looks as though it were built before the start of the 19th century. There are no suburbs. The city just suddenly appears out of the haze, low, flat and compact, made exclusively of mud, as if it were a young island struggling to reach some sunlight. It is in danger of being swallowed by the harmattan, the dry wind that constantly blows from east to west, layering everything with a permanent coating that feels like sandpaper. It looks today as it probably did during the time of Marco Polo.

Since these words were written numerous Taureg fighters who went to Libya for the insurrection against the Kaddafi regime fought and returned home with sophisticated weapons for the first time that allowed them to overthrow the ruling Malian government that had suppressed them for so long. They hardly had time to celebrate before factions of Al-Queda moved into the breach and forced the very unorganized Tuareg fighters into an ever smaller corner of northern Mali, with many fleeing to refugee camps in Burkina Faso.

During this time, Al Queda set about systematically blowing up numerous religious sites and graves of holy men, specifically 300 revered Sufi sites, in and around Timbuktu in an all-out terror campaign designed to shock and awe the simple desert people, cowing them into total submission. Halis fled to a refugee camp where he contacted me by e-mail and gave me steady updates on what was happening. When I last heard from Him, he had taken refuge in Colorado with his American born wife but planned to return to Timbuktu in hopes of retrieving his property and seeing if the hotel he managed before the invasion was still standing.

I have been unable to contact him since then.

INTO THE SAHARA

The blowing sand rocks our Land Rover as we reach the outskirts of Timbuktu.

Mahmoud leans over the steering wheel and peers into the hazy lemon yellow that fills our windshield. There is no horizon between earth and sky and I wonder how he can continue to drive with no reference points, yet on he goes with the instinct of a desert nomad. I realize for him, this is normal.

He tells me these storms can last for days but I do not care. We have finally reached one of the oldest and most remote cities on earth, so let it blow. I have traveled this far to enter the world of the Blue Men, lords of the Sahara, and it is too late to alter any plans.

The trouble with trans-Atlantic flights is that they give you plenty of time to think and on this one my thoughts recalled the journey of Sir Richard Burton who disguised as a wandering beggar, became the first white outsider to enter Mecca as a pilgrim in 1852. Had he been discovered, he would have forfeited his life. While I had no illusions of my trip being anywhere near as dangerous as that of Sir Richard, it was still pushing the envelope a bit. I am after all, an infidel.

My Tuareg contact, Halis, was tall and dignified with an air of self-confidence that precedes him. His blue robes were trimmed with gold denoting his standing within the Tuareg hierarchy, and he wears the silver medallion around his neck the Berbers refer to as their passport, a talisman that wards off evil while announcing the travelers' native village. His word puts me at ease regarding my acceptance or rejection by his fellow tribesmen, informing me they would consider my dressing as one of them to be a compliment. He also informed me I need not worry about bandits while traveling as a Tuareg.

I did not know what this meant until he pointed at the wall map to his home village of Arawan, a former Foreign Legion outpost, north of Timbuktu in the trackless Sahara. It sits in an area most guidebooks call

"Bandit Country." It is the only speck on the map for 120 miles in every direction.

Halis has shrugged off my query about bandits, saying they fear Tuaregs. My own paranoia will have to decide if this is simply his hubris, or a statement of fact. I am going into the deep desert not only with, but dressed as a Berber nomad.

Early the following morning we awake early and I stumble into the hazy morning light in my blue robes to find a waiting Land Rover. What have I done?

There are no roads and few trees, only low scrub brush and moving dunes. Tuareg boys learn every star in the heavens and can easily navigate by them, but when I ask how he does this by day, Mahmoud points to a tree and says, "That is where we ate spaghetti," and at another saying, "That is where we camped with the Germans." He knows every natural formation like I know my living room, because this is his.

We barrel along at thirty miles an hour, our wheels sometimes airborne, and Mahmoud smiling like some demented Parnelli Jones. He is having a great time while I must blank my mind to the obvious fact that if we break down here it could be days before anyone finds us. He and Halis frequently argue in French and I am later told this is over Mahmouds' choice of trails. Halis feels we are better off sticking to established tire tracks while Mahmoud prefers to blaze his own way. All I can do is try not to think of broken axles.

At one point we crest an enormous dune and Mahmoud tells me to get out and walk down in case he rolls the car. I am about to do so when I realize that would mean I am alone and on foot in the Sahara. I refuse and tell him why. He laughs, and with a loud throaty scream guns the engine sending us hurtling down a 100 foot wave of flowing sand, covering us in the process and forcing me to restart my heart.

Time and again, we "surf" the dunes and I finally learn to relax and trust his expert touch as we career downhill at various weird angles.

After four hours we stop under a stunted mesquite and within seconds Mahmoud has a fire going from broken branches after producing a spark with flint and adze while the wind howls around him. In this weather, I could not produce a fire with a lighter and gasoline, but he has done it as his forefathers have for a thousand years. Minutes later we are sipping our hot sweet tea and eating tinned sardines. I sit with my back to the wind marveling that Halis and Mahmoud are comfortable in these conditions. When I stand up two minutes later, I leave a two foot berm that has stacked up against my prone body.

After four more hours of trackless bouncing and sliding through loose sand we see the outlines of low squat buildings in the haze before us. The wind has never stopped blowing and we have reached Arawan.

I am anxious about our reception as I step into the maelstrom in my blue robes. I am instantly greeted by the outstretched hands of the village elder, Halis' uncle, who takes me into a low adobe for more tea. The building is pockmarked with bullet holes from a time when the Legion ruled this country with an iron fist. He tells me a visitor honors the Tuareg when they wear the robes, and I am the first outsider his nephew has brought to this village.

As I sip my tea, young men in indigo turbans file silently into the room to have a look at this strange westerner who would live among them. After greetings, a communal rice bowl appears with cubes of seared beef. The woman who serves it never lifts her eyes and exits the room quickly in one smooth motion. As an honored guest, I must eat first and am careful to follow Islamic tradition by scooping only with the fingers of my right hand. I smack my lips loudly to show approval and quickly pass off the bowl to hungry faces lining the wall, knowing the children outside will only get to eat what I and the other men do not. As for the women, that is a world totally closed to me.

Halis calls me outside, yelling with excitement and pointing at a long black line on the horizon. A caravan is approaching and it appears to be a big one. Running over the dunes is very slow going for the two miles to the well where the weary drivers will allow their beasts to stop.

Arriving with the first camels, their nomad handlers are startled to see a Tuareg wielding cameras, running in and out of their charges like a gleeful child. I run between long lines of Dromedary camels, (one hump) each carrying a handmade wooden rack on which is hung four tremendous

blocks of salt weighing about 200 pounds a block. Animals skins are slung between the blocks to act as buffers, and on top, numerous smaller slabs of salt are tied with rope to the carrying rack. The camels lumber on ignoring me as I dash through their ranks, beside myself in disbelief at this photographic opportunity.

Each camel is tethered to the tail of the one in front of him by a nose halter allowing one or two drivers to control more than 200 of them at a time. They move at a slow and steady gate, chewing their cuds as they lumber on.

This strip of the southern Sahara has been a caravan route at least since the time of Jesus. The men and boys driving these camels were born to this as were their fathers and great, great grandfathers. Halis will later tell me a Tuareg boy must make this trip at least once to be counted a man, and he himself has done it seven times. Salt was once money in this part of the world and is still a valued commodity, so much so that those not willing to mine it are more than willing to take it at gun point. Two of the drivers carry ancient muzzle loading rifles that would be more at home in a museum, yet out here may be the difference between life and death.

The camels are halted and their tenders begin the arduous task of unloading the heavy salt blocks. Each camel sits with its legs folded underneath waiting to have its burden temporarily lifted, protesting every human touch with the most foul sounding guttural noises. They are left untethered for they have nowhere to go and will not leave their food source.

Long sprouts of grain are spread on the sand for them to eat but they will get no water. Having just drunk three days prior, it would be a waste at this point. Halis says the camels can go three weeks without water this time of year but when it gets hotter they must drink every week. When they do drink, they will consume 100 gallons of water in 10 minutes.

The camel is a perfectly adapted creature that carries unbelievable loads up to 40 miles a day. When they rest on the hot sand, hard calluses on their elbows and knees keep them from burning. Their nostrils lock shut and their long lashes protect their eyes from blowing sand over their nictitating membranes that allow them to see in the fiercest of dust storms. They store fat in their hump, not water as is commonly believed, and have extra thick lips to allow the ingestion of thorny desert plants. When times are tough, they have been known to eat animal skin and bones and can digest almost anything. They are indeed, "ships of the desert "and one tries to bite me when I get too close, proving what I have heard about their nasty temperament. They can also spray their urine with deadly accuracy.

With the wind increasing I fear becoming lost in a white out. I am almost two miles from Arawan and have limited vision. I tuck my cameras under my robes and put my head down into the wind, making for the nearest shelter before it is too late.

When I return the sun is setting and a small fire is burning between two buildings. Tea is on the brazier and the evenings story telling has already begun. I sit with my back to a wall and watch the firelight dance on the faces around me. They are faces out of the bible, ancient, weathered and wise. Tea is passed around and pipes are lit. Looking up at the stars I realize this scene would be no different if it took place a millenium ago.

OF NOMADS AND WHALES

From the back of a camel the Sahara seemed endless; an infinite sea of low rolling dunes baked by an ever present sun that sucks all moisture out of any creature it can reach.

For one month I had been immersed in Berber Tuareg culture, traveling through Mali, as one of the famed blue men, on the trans-Saharan caravan routes they had operated for over 2000 years. We carried no maps, GPS, or satellite phones, navigating only by landmarks, intuition, and the inbred sense of direction that is part of nomadic DNA. They were fierce desert warriors, straight out of central casting, lords of the desert; the bane of any bandits who crossed their path, and they had allowed me to enter their world.

Halis arranged for his cousin, Mahmoud, to drive us into the desert where we would meet our mounts, and I found Mahmoud to be a friendly but somewhat feral man whose scarred face betrayed a hard life. In the days ahead I learned that he slept with one eye open and his knife half drawn at the hint of any intrusion, deciding that in the desert, these were admirable qualities. In their combined company I felt secure because when a Tuareg gives his word, he will die for it. We drove from Timbuktu to the crumbling former foreign legion outpost of Arawan, about 100 miles north, now a watering stop for caravans hauling salt from the northern mines near Tademmi, south to Timbuktu. Stepping out of the Land Rover in my blue robes, I was welcomed by a young Tuareg who simply walked over to me and with a slight bow, handed me the reign to a camel.

That evening I sat around a small fire, wrapped in blue and surrounded by sons of the desert, eating seared goat and rice with our fingers in a scene unchanged since the time of Christ. Except for Halis, they spoke their native Tamasheq and a few spoke French while I spoke neither and did not care. They were men of few words and I needed none. I had entered a society I had thought closed to me and was absorbed in the moment.

The following morning we left by camel to complete a wide arcing circle of the southern Sahara, visiting numerous nomad camps along the way.

By the end of the first day my camel had already bitten me on the leg and showered me with his urine, but I learned quickly how to control him and was soon mounting and dismounting as though born to it. At each new nomad camp I was immediately served sweet tea as custom demands, and taken to see the head man, and always treated as a Tuareg without reservation.

I expected at all times to be inundated with questions about the outside world, especially about the United States, but realized these people live such an isolated existence that their world and curiosity extended no further than the immediate needs of the day. Where I came from and who I was did not matter. The term America had no meaning for them. I was just an outsider from many days ride away, who had joined the tribe, helping with daily chores, tending to camels, and listening to ancient tales around the occasional evening camp fire. I slept the peaceful sleep of the dead, rolled in my robes, under the desert stars that Leo Africanus laid under.

The contrast with my own society was overwhelming. While those of us who live in the west spend most of our waking hours in offices or on computers, these people found joy in the tiniest, most intimate moments, particularly in relating funny stories or retelling oral histories. It was a simplistic life, free of stress and full of laughter, a daily search for the spiritual and a way of life unchanged for two millenniums. By the end of the second day, I was already questioning my own material values.

Though they were primarily Muslims, they had no reservations about having this Christian infidel in their midst. I was just another traveler, and the law of the desert required them to offer me hospitality which they did freely. I found this to be more Christian like than many who simply professed that faith without applying right actions.

It struck me that I never saw any of them openly praying as I had expected, and when I finally got the nerve to approach the subject with Halis, he patted his heart and said "God lives within here. I pray all day long." When I told him that was my own approach to religion, he just smiled lightly and said, "I know."

On our final day, the three of us were approaching the outskirts of Timbuktu, Halis looking every inch the Tuareg nobleman on his amber colored camel, myself in the middle, and Mahmoud; hand on his dagger hilt, scanning left and right for trouble.

I spotted a man standing on a wall, spotlessly dressed head to toe like an ad for REI. The two cameras around his neck identified him as a tourist, and he was raising his long lens directly towards us. Without thinking I held up my hand and called loudly, "Cadou! Cadou!" meaning, "Give me money if you want my photograph." It was common enough among poor local people to ask for a few coins in such a situation, but why I did it so reflexively I just cannot say, other than I was caught up in the moment.

Halis immediately picked up on what I was doing and began to laugh softly under his tagelmoust.

The startled photographer jumped off the wall, fumbling through his pockets, then shyly approached me with a coin. I made a great show of examining it, holding it up to the light, and even biting it as I had seen in a movie long ago. Finally tucking it into the folds of my robe, I stood tall in the saddle, striking my best warrior pose and said, "OK, take photo!" The man clicked away as the three of us rode past him, with Halis no longer able to control his laughter and even Mahmoud giggling under his breath.

That poor gentleman who thought he had just taken a National Geographic photo of a lord of the desert will never know he had just shot a middle aged white guy from Los Angeles.

The three of us arrived at my hotel, laughing so hard that tears now streaked Halis' face. We parted ways with plans to re-unite that evening for a farewell dinner, my thank you for such an amazing journey, and I spent most of the afternoon thinking of a proper tip to give Halis and Mahmoud, realizing they most likely would prefer receiving a goat instead of money, when a truly original idea struck me.

I was carrying a portable hard drive full of photos of whales I had taken on a previous trip to Mexico. I doubted either of these desert nomads who lived in a land locked country had ever seen the ocean let along a whale, so when they arrived I plugged my hard drive into the tiny 12 inch black and white television and there in a Timbuktu hotel, proceeded to show them dozens of whale photos.

These two hardened warriors, with daggers stuck in their waist bands, sat cross legged on my bed, giggling like small children at recess, yelling at each new image, pointing at the screen, and poking each other with unabashed glee. They bounced up and down and I was overjoyed at their unexpected exuberance. They were particularly taken with the shots of 40 ton whales breaching, and asked how could they do this?

With nothing to compare this to they called them big fish, and when they asked how large they really were, I recalled that we had crossed the Niger river together and had seen hippopotamus; I added that the whales were many times larger than hippos, but am not sure they believed me.

They stared in open mouthed amazement, not only at the photos of whales, but equally at the fact that I could put such pictures on an electronic screen. For these men who mixed Islam with superstition, desert myth, and ancient ceremony, what I was giving them was tantamount to magic.

We were having such a great time that when we finished, the local restaurants were closed but it did not matter. We all embraced with oaths of eternal friendship and I watched as they walked off into the humid night, chattering like jaybirds until becoming silhouettes against the mud city.

I went to my bed smiling, grateful for the surreal worlds we had introduced each other to, and felt it was a great exchange.

BEGGING FOR AN EDUCATION

My friend, Noah, and I were driving along a remote road in Benin, West Africa, when we passed a group of young boys. From a distance they appeared to be a rag tag bunch, maybe a gang, and I gave them little thought until Noah pulled the car over and said, "You should talk to these boys."

Up close I could see they were rather well dressed and groomed, ranging in age from about six to13 years, and I could not imagine why he wanted me to speak with them, feeling especially vulnerable since I could see no one else around for miles.

They crowded around, as curious about me as I was of them, and through Noah they told me that in this part of Africa, a child really is raised by the entire village, and if one did not have the means to support everybody, some of the children were designated to leave with the blessings of all adults. It became their job to wander from village to village, begging as a group. Begging there carries no social stigma and is accepted as any other form of meaningful employment. Children are simply better at it than the elderly and so it becomes a full time job. Such groups of children are actually a common sight throughout this part of the world.

I might add that none of these boys ever asked me for money.

Older children are put in charge of younger ones, just as at home, making sure they do all necessary things such as brushing their teeth and washing their clothes.

Most importantly, they have a code of honor. They do not lie or steal, and they all share whatever they take in with each other. At this point, the youngest boy who was beaming with a mile wide smile obviously had something he was proud of and reaching into his backpack he pulled out a wooden tablet to show me.

In most of rural Africa there is little paper and fewer pens or pencils. Families will carve a small wooden tablet for writing, the size of a notebook that is passed down from one generation to the next. Ink is made from the ashes of a fire mixed with water and a river reed serves as a pen. The children write their lessons on them each day and wash them clean in a river at night for use again the following day.

This is what children use in school, and it is what each of these young beggars carried in his backpack.

This young man told me they had all done their lessons early in the morning before the heat and the day's travels, and added that one day he hoped to become a teacher himself. Another boy showed me his tablet and said he was going to be a doctor, while another wanted to become a veterinarian. They all said this matter of fact as though it were already a done deal for each of them.

He told me they loved being outside rather than in the confines of a building, that they were learning about the environment first hand this way and felt that being out in the middle of everyday life was a better education than any they could receive in their respective villages.

I was overwhelmed by the upbeat nature of this young man and his companions, and everything he said made perfect sense to me. If itinerant beggars could hold such large dreams, then I felt the future of Africa was in good hands.

Before I left, the oldest boy asked me if there were any beggars in America or if everyone was rich. When I told him there were many beggars he thought I was making a joke at first. Then he asked how these beggars were treated and I told him that most people walked past them pretending as if they were not there. I tried to explain that there were simply too many poor people to stop and give something to everyone of them.

None of the boys believed me.

TO FIND A KING

Several years ago in Africa, I met a king.

Africa has many kings, some self- proclaimed, while others are hereditary, and they run the gamut from despot to enlightened ruler.

I have met more than a few in my travels, but had never before sought one out.
The oral histories of Africa allow for personal interpretation, and stories of great men usually carry much embellishment creating a chasm between the myth and the man. The stories I heard of this king could only be called legendary; that he was a shape shifter, assuming the guise of a panther at night. Some said he could fly, talk to animals, and was wise beyond belief. They also said he was still a boy. Such a story begs to be followed.

Centuries ago the Kaan or Gan people, (pronounced Goon) depending on who is doing the spelling, migrated from Ghana into what is today the southwestern corner of Burkina Faso in West Africa, settling near Loropini. They number less than six thousand.

They are primarily animists and practitioners of voodoo that permeates most West African cultures. Their king is elected from and by members of the royal family, rules for life, and is the keeper of traditional fetishes that are the soul of Gan beliefs. Some say this king took the throne at age eleven, with worldly insight that far exceeded his isolated existence. Theirs is an ancient culture.

Monsoon clogged roads forced me to abandon my vehicle forcing an eight mile trek through dried millet fields where I accidentally stumbled into the voodoo soul of the Gan, a re-created burial ground as it were, with stone houses, each containing a clay effigy of a seated former king, inlaid with cowry shell eyes and mouth. At first, in the darkness, I thought I was viewing mummies lifelike enough to stand and accost me. This was the Gan place of ritual and source of the king's power. It is here that he comes for the advice of his ancestors when the mantle of rule proves too heavy to bear. I did not linger, for in many tribal areas, violating a burial ground is a serious offense. I left an offering of salt, more for the benefit of prying eyes than my own beliefs.

Not far away I saw his majesty sitting placidly in a wooden deck chair under a shade tree.

He was not a boy, but not yet fully a man either. His ebony skin was flawless and he had long thin fingers that would be at home on a piano keyboard, locked in clenched fists under his chin as though deep in thought. His long caftan and skull cap did not betray his status, and none of the ostentatious trappings that usually accompany African royalty were in evidence. He turned to offer a slight smile at my approach, saying in French, "I knew you were coming father."

That simple phrase alluded to psychic abilities, but I knew countless people had seen me fighting through the brush, and no doubt the "jungle telegraph" had warned him of my arrival; still, this announcement added to his mystique of special knowledge while throwing me off balance.

In Africa my white hair has often given me entre to villages normally closed to outsiders because there, more than anyplace on earth, age demands respect. The longer you live the more knowledge you accumulate, and education is at a premium. In remote villages, I am usually older than any of the chiefs. I take full advantage of my age in such situations to see places and seek answers not available to a younger man.

He motioned me to a bench in front of him while a lady approached from a nearby hut. She sat at his side with her hand on his shoulder and introduced herself in English as his fourth wife and thus a queen. The king spoke directly to me in his native tongue, his black eyes never wavering in their stare, while his wife explained that he was in mourning for the death of one of his three other wives and not in the best of spirits, but his quick smile did not betray any such emotion.
I spoke with him, through her, of all manner of topics, from African politics to the health of our families. When I asked his name I was told I would not be able to pronounce it, and that his true name was known only to his people, for such knowledge in the hands of his enemies could harm him. Such is voodoo.

I asked what he thought of America having a black president and he laughed, saying Africa had been ruled by black men for centuries and America was just now catching up. He wisely added that it was our fate to be ruled by black men as we had originally brought them to America as slaves and were now receiving our due. I held my tongue by not reminding him that it was the black kings of Africa who rounded up their own people to sell to white slavers, but I was not there for confrontation. I wanted to know his thoughts.

We talked of philosophy, religion, and at one point he asked me what snow was like, having never known cold.

His questions came from a separate reality than my own and I found him fascinating, but in no way did I think of him as great. In Africa where rulers are most often despots, such a benign and friendly ruler could certainly be perceived as great to his own people and that is how legends begin. I even thought that perhaps in another time and place we might become friends.

We talked throughout the afternoon and not wishing to overstay my welcome, and with no offer to stay in his village overnight, I said I must go.

His majesty beckoned me to follow and there behind some bushes sat a decrepit 66 Nissan sedan that did not appear to be in running condition but the king got in, started the engine, belching black smoke everywhere, and beckoned for me to join him. He was personally going to drive me back to my vehicle. With the roads clogged by mud we veered across millet fields, bounding over uneven ground as fast as the king could coax his aging wheels to go. I hung on for dear life, with no seat belt, as my head met the ceiling more than once. Seeing the broad smile on his face I realized he was having a wonderful time and let my own apprehension go, enjoying the wildest ride I ever had.

In the village, surrounded by his people, he was the noble leader, but here in the bush, behind the wheel of his car, he could be the young boy that still resided in the man's body. This was his relief from the prison of rule and I was his excuse. Two different cultures had merged into the kind of day a traveler can only hope for.

We passed startled villagers, wide eyed and open mouthed, as they watched this strange white intruder bouncing along in the king's car, many of them bowing as we passed, but most too startled to move. I have no doubt that at that moment I became a story to be told around their evening meal for generations.

We broke through into a clearing and saw my vehicle ahead, finally coming to a halt with a sliding, brake wrenching stop. His majesty just turned and smiled, gesturing towards my vehicle as calmly as if asking me to lunch. He posed for a final picture and then reached under his robe to hand me a small slip of paper. It was a Xerox with his photo on it and read, 'His Majesty, the 29th King of the Gan." It also had a cell phone number. So there under the broiling African sun, I exchanged business cards with a king and got into my own vehicle, watching as he put the Nissan into reverse and backed away with all the élan that had brought us here.

I have often thought about that encounter and of the two sides of the person I had found; a young man who inspired a legend. It is then that I think of calling his cell phone but know the call would not go through, nor would he remember me even if I could speak his tongue.

Almost two years later I received an e-mail from him, as he apparently just got internet service, from who knows where. He asked if we could correspond and so now I have an African king for a pen pal. He writes to me often and we talk of people, love, life, death, and God, and I am grateful for such a rare gift.

I had become a story for his village, and now he is mine.

MY FRIEND MOSES

Travel does not always begin with the boarding of an airplane, but rather at the moment one opens the mind to new possibilities and that is why I was quite surprised when the gentleman I had engaged in dinner conversation at a party in Los Angeles told me he was an elder of the Maasai nation.

Moses was in America to study theology at a local seminary, very contrary for the traditional Maasai who, as animists, shun western style education. When finished, he would be only the sixth Maasai known to receive a PHD. While still engaged in his studies he shuttled back and forth between America and Kenya where he had created a foundation that drills water wells and builds schools in the bush.

After a year of invitations, my wife and I found ourselves on a hot, dusty Africa savannah and the culture shock was complete when I saw Moses, normally clad in blue jeans and a blazer, in his brilliant red shuka, (Maasai robe) with a long spear. The only familiar connection was his brilliant smile as I saw my old friend for the first time in his natural state, a man of power and respect within his own element.

We spent that first afternoon walking through his valley while Moses spun tales of growing up with wild animals for companions and not hearing a mechanical sound until he was almost ten years old. Suddenly he motioned towards a tree where a young leopard sat eyeing us, and at that point, Africa became a very serious place.
The Maasai have a connection to the earth that is beyond the comprehension of those of us who dwell in cities; it is their home and mother. For them there is no afterlife; you simply return to the earth. There is no past or future, only the now, and they live accordingly as stewards of the earth.

He told us how to track an animal, how to read its scat, and know its sex by the depth of its print in the dirt. He showed us how to follow a trail by the bend of a leaf, and I realized that while in Africa, he occupied a separate reality than I did, and marveled at how he transitioned from one to the other with ease.

He spoke of how as traditional nomads, he was never sure where his family would be when he returned to Africa, and would wander the valley till he found them.   We walked for hours and I asked him how the Maasai navigate in the bush. Moses just smiled and said, a Maasai may not always know where he is, but he is never lost. When we returned to the village he invited us inside his hut and became very serious, asking if we wanted to know about hunting lions.

Lion hunting has long been central to Maasai culture. In olden days, before a Maasai boy could be considered a man, he had to participate in a lion hunt using only a spear and animal hide shield. The first lion hunt was the paramount point in the life of a Maasai youth, and nothing he did for the rest of his life would equal its importance.

Even though this practice was outlawed by the Kenyan government long ago, the Maasai still practice it covertly, and Moses was being unusually candid by his willingness to share such intimate information.

He stared into the fire for a long time before speaking, and I knew this story would be a rare gift to a friend. The word friend has special meaning to the Maasai, much more than in western society. To them it is more like being a brother, and when Moses applied it to me, it touched my soul.

Moses was 13 when he was picked for his first lion hunt, determined to prove himself and gain great face, but admitted to such fear that he could not sleep the night before the hunt.

On the actual morning, while his face was being painted as a warrior for the first time, he felt everyone could hear his heart pounding, and was sure all would notice the spear shaking in his hand. As the warriors gathered in the morning mist, his knees almost buckled.

The Maasai hunt a lion by forming a circle around it and then slowly walk forward, tightening the circle. Eventually the lion will feel cornered and spring at one man who is supposed to drop to the ground, cover himself with his shield, and hope his fellow warriors kill the lion before it kills him.

With a grand gesture Moses reached down and pulled up his shuka, revealing a long jagged scar running for several inches along his lower leg. He stared at the scar for several seconds before saying in a very soft voice

"From my first lion hunt!"

Amazed he had survived such an attack I blurted out, "The lion did that to you?"
Moses looked me square in the eye and said, "No, I was so scared I speared myself in the leg, and the lion got away!" and with that he threw his head back and laughed. To this day, Moses has never killed a lion.

As rare guests we dined on goat that evening while a chorus of cicadas announced the coming of the African night, and I pondered how my western girth would fit inside one of their tiny huts whose sleeping compartments resemble those of a working man's hotel in Tokyo, much like sliding into a bee hive. When I expressed this concern to Moses he pointed just outside the thorn bush wall that surrounds the village where two of his nephews were wrestling with a nylon tent. He was way ahead of me.

Grateful as I was for this comfort, I expressed concern to Moses about sleeping outside the thorn wall with the image of a leopard still fresh in my mind. The Maasai fear leopards more than lions because a lion will make a kill and eat it while a leopard will kill everything in sight before it settles down to eat. Before leaving he smiled and said not "if" but "when" the leopard comes, we need only yell and a dozen warriors would come running with spears. Before I could raise an objection to his certainty of our receiving a visit from a mass killer he put his hand on my shoulder and said not to worry as the leopard would not like our smell, and with that he walked off, secure in his pronouncement.

No sooner were Irene and I inside the tent than most of the village had surrounded us, pulling the zipper up and down while running their hands over the strange new sensation of nylon. Most of them had never seen a tent before, and called it an "instant hut."

A full moon was rising over the tree line, and it turned the silhouettes of our curious visitors into an ongoing puppet show crawling over our tent walls as they continued to play with the zipper and occasionally thrust an ebony head inside to giggle at us strange creatures.

Surreal patterns glided over the tent wall as tiny fingers and old hands ran up and down. We were as much an oddity as a circus act and at first we stayed inside hoping to minimize our impact, but this only fed the people's

curiosity as more and more poked their heads inside for a brief glimpse of us. This went on until I stepped outside to see just how many people there were who had yet to pay us a visit.

To my surprise a line of people snaked through the forest and down into the valley where word had spread about these visitors and their instant hut, and now the entire valley was migrating towards our tent. As far as I could see, Maasai were coming from all around to see us.

Irene stepped outside to greet our visitors. Most shook our hands while others simply wanted to touch us. For some, we would be the only white people they would ever know. No one spoke and there was no need for words. In that magical evening we were all simply people, coming together to meet each other for the first and only time, frozen by a human touch that instantly passed into memory.

I went back inside the tent, lying next to Irene and watched this never ending procession of shadows through the night. There would be no sleep and we did not care. No festival, ceremony, or dance could have been more entertaining or enlightening to us. The Maasai are story tellers, and in Africa, especially among tribes with no written language, stories quickly become both history and legend. Stories tend to grow with each telling and take on the flavor of the narrator.

I know that evening we became a story to be told around their campfires for a very long time.

DANCING WITH THE DEAD

I had never been confronted by a dead man before, and have to admit at the moment we came face to face, I was more concerned with getting the shot than my own demise.

Without warning a whirling dervish of Egun rushed in my direction stopping only at the final second, perhaps unnerved since I did not scream and flee as the other villagers did at such a moment. I was absorbed in taking photos and stood my ground, never thinking for a moment that my life was in peril, but as the dancer put on the brakes, his long robes kept coming, flowing over me like an ocean wave and an audible collective gasp went through the crowd. I had been touched by the living dead, and to the audience, like a scene from the movie, "Ghost," the spirits were now on their way to collect my soul. The young apprentice who should have shielded me had frozen and just stood there, his mouth agape, unable to comprehend why an outsider would be sought out for this.

It took a few seconds before I heard the utter silence, and from the corner of my eye I saw an older man, swathed in purple and holding a staff that announced his position within the hierarchy of the mambos, jump to his feet and begin issuing orders to others.

A man rushed to my side, holding what looked like a wand in his hand and proceeded to wave it over my body much like a hand held metal detector at an airport. As he did this his eyes were rolled back in his head and he appeared to be in a state of trance, mumbling incantations. Just like that I had gone from spectator to victim.

The muse had called me to the tiny village of Cove' in Benin, Africa, where I had been told I might witness an Egun Gun dance, (Pronounced Egoon Goon) one of the more esoteric of all voodoo events. It is this dance more than any other ceremony that merges the living with the dead, but I, being counted among the living, had not planned on merging before it happened.

Voodoo is a word that frightens most people, mainly because it is misunderstood. It conjures up images of zombies, black magic, and dolls with pins stuck in them, and while that does play a role in the overall milieu, there is much more to it than that.

It is in fact, an established religion whose oral histories can be traced back 6,000 years to Benin, where it is still the official religion of the country, and an estimated 60% of all West African inhabitants practice it in one form or another.

The origins of black magic voodoo go back some 300 years when the black kings of Africa hunted their own people, selling them to white slavers. In the hulls of slave ships the evolution of dark voodoo took root as the only means of fighting back. By the time these ships reached the Caribbean, a benign belief system had been distorted into a darker art that grew and spread in its' new homeland, eventually reaching all the way to New Orleans, USA.

To the adherents of traditional African voodoo there is no difference between the waking world and that of spirits, they are the same, co-existing in what a westerner might call a parallel universe. The living and the dead are in constant communion, aiding each other just as they did in physical life. It is the job of the mambo, the West African version of a priest, to oversee this union, to guide it using established traditions that allow the living to navigate among the dead without being totally drawn into that void. While they believe the deceased are constantly among us, they also believe a living person can enter the twilight world for brief periods if under careful guidance, and of course depending on the personal power of the metaphysical traveler. The witch doctor or shaman are nothing more than spiritual guides who facilitate communication between those who have gone before and those who still occupy the material world.

The ceremony is presided over by a council of mambos as they are known locally; there are usually several in attendance, but the uninitiated will not know who they are. They are secret masters of ceremony, plainly dressed to blend in, making sure all goes according to plan, and ready to make judgment calls if things get out of hand, as I was about to find out.

The Egun Gun are a secret society of men who spend most of their adult life learning an archaic set of rituals, prayers, and ceremonial traditions, that include their own private language and dances. They spend great amounts of time creating surreal looking outfits that hide not only their true identity, but emphasize the fact that the wearer is in a special place and not of this world.

They are so secretive that fellow tribal members do not know who is a member or not, and that days before a ceremony an Egun Gun dancer secretes his homemade ceremonial costume in the woods and makes excuses to disappear so no one will know where he is going and no one will ask or wonder why. During this time he prepares himself through fasting and prayer. Even more fascinating is the fact that once the ritual begins, he becomes a channel for the living dead.

The Egun dance is tradition and religious rite simultaneously; as much theater as ceremony, part Kabuki and part melodrama, but deadly serious.

Once in costume and mask the dancer is no longer a member of the material world. He enters a trance like state, becoming a conduit for a deceased relative to enter his body. When this is achieved the dancer will begin to gyrate and contort in ways not normally doable in a waking state. The idea is that the dancer mimics all he has seen from his fellow tribesmen during the period since the last dance, showing the spirit inside him what everyone has done lately. This in turn allows the spirit to know who has been good or bad and who needs to be punished or rewarded.

Ancestors, who are never far away, are the keepers and arbitrators of how their families should live and this dance is their opportunity to do a periodic checkup. But being spirits, benign or not, they all hold a "terribelita" that once unleashed could wreak havoc if not properly controlled by ceremony.

With their elaborately colored costumes and flowing robes, the Egun Gun twirl and jump, jerk and swoon, then randomly pick a person from the gathered crowd, directed from the spirit within, and race headlong at them, adding drama to the moment and also panic because it is believed that if the dancer touches you, your physical body will soon wither and die and you will be transported into the spirit world.

To assure no physical contact is made, young apprentices accompany each dancer using a long bamboo rod which they use to poke those they think are too close, imposing themselves between the dancer and the crowd, and apparently immune to the lethal contact due to their station. As a guest I had a young boy at my side for just this reason who failed in his task.

Now, I was in effect, receiving an exorcism, and a local man who spoke English came forward to explain to me that the wand the mambo was using was the femur of a lion, killed by a warrior with a spear, thus infusing it with power sufficient to ward off my imminent departure from this earth. It was inlaid with several dozen cowry shells; a common adornment used throughout Africa, representing fertility because of their resemblance to a vagina and thus were an affirmation of life and a strong deterrent to my current dilemma.

I was told to stand still as the bone was passed over my body, drawing the evil spirits from inside and corralling them inside the shell openings, pulling them out and passing them into the ether where they were harmlessly dispersed to seek another venue to invade.

I believe there is power in voodoo, but for it to have dominion, the practitioner must also have belief in it, and while I am open to esoteric beliefs more than most people, I had no fear for my life in spite of what was happening. I have my own religious convictions, thus rendering it impotent against me, but I also understand the collective power of belief, and I was surrounded by a crowd of adherents who were firmly convinced that I was in imminent danger, so out of respect for them, I continued my role in the ceremony. After all, how many people get to experience a real live voodoo exorcism?

When he finished, the mambo dropped the lion bone, saying he could no longer hold it because its soul was too heavy, and he himself appeared physically spent, staggering back to join his compatriots on the arm of a young assistant. Only then did the head mambo retake his seat.

It was explained that I had been turned free by the spirits that had entered my body, and that I must have a great power since I was still alive where one of the local villagers could not have survived such an invasion. In fact, had it been one of them, the mambo would not have even tried to intervene. These newly minted spirits would be able to return during the next dance, just not in a living body. It was also explained that a cleansing ceremony would be performed later to restore the lion bone to its original condition as a talisman of power before it could re-instate the authority of its owner.

To the assembled crowd, I had spent a few seconds suspended between the two worlds and so had gained a new status. It sounded like one of those stories of people close to death describing a white light at the end of a tunnel and then being drawn back to the present although I had no such experience. It was imposed upon me by those watching the ceremony.

At this point the villagers were gathering around me, touching me, grabbing my hands. Most were smiling but a few shed tears as my experience had apparently elevated me to a spiritual state I was not aware of, and had given me great face with the community.

In Africa, children often bow to an elder for a blessing, bestowed by the simple touch of one's palm laid flat on the crown of the head. Several mothers brought their infants to me for this blessing, now instilled with new meaning by my supposed conquest of the evil.

I had originally intended to stay a couple days to observe these ceremonies, and had I decided to do so I no doubt would have been treated as an honored guest, but that did not seem right for something that was imposed on me and I had not earned.

With great humility I bid my farewell to all, profusely thanking the mambos for saving me great suffering, and walked through an admiring crowd, shaking hands all the way to my vehicle. I heard the word mambo muttered by several people and realized they now meant me. Never would I have expected the experience I had that day, prompted by a simple photo shoot, and knew that few outsiders would ever be drawn into the secret world of voodoo in such a manner.

In Africa, events are always stories, stories soon become myth, and myth often becomes a legend.

Perhaps one day I will be sitting at a campfire in West Africa and hear the story of the white mambo who entered the spirit world and returned.

THE BIRD MAN OF CAIRO

I have always considered it a rare treat to be invited into a local home in a foreign country.

When our guide in Egypt issued such an invitation, (You must meet my father, he is old like you!) Irene and I jumped at the opportunity. That is how we met Ahmed Bahaa, world class pigeon racer.

Pigeon racing is a little known sport in America, but in Europe and parts of North Africa, it has long had a great following. Driving through dark back streets, and climbing four unlit flights of stairs, I began to feel a bit like Indiana Jones, and wondered if we had made a serious mistake in accepting this offer.

When the door opened, we were greeted by the kindly Mrs. Bahaa, a beautiful elder wrapped head to toe in traditional dress who averted her eyes and quickly disappeared after meeting us.

We stepped into an apartment the size of a large closet, with walls covered by certificates and trophies.

"Come and meet my children" announced a voice from the balcony, and wandering outside I was met with a very wet kiss on both cheeks by the man himself, who immediately declared us to be family, and told us this was our home whenever we are in Cairo. Now that is not bad for someone you have just met.

Ahmed Bahaa is a retired importer/exporter and full time pigeon racer, who loves life, a good story, and we would quickly find out, a good joke.

After freeing myself from his bear hug, I realized we were surrounded by pigeons, roosting in an area the size of my hall way. In all, Mr. Bahaa keeps almost 200 pigeons on his tiny balcony, in a space most neighbors in America would soon begin to complain about. I must also add that it was totally spotless and odorless. Birds are this man's passion.

We were immediately covered with curious pigeons, all coming to greet their new visitors, and had to shuffle our feet in order not to trample any.

Without further ado, Mr. Bahaa began to grab pigeons from their roosts, introducing each of them to us in a booming voice that belied his 78 years and could be heard by most of the neighborhood.

We met champions from international races, young birds in training, and his main stud bird. Each one was named and he could identify them from a hundred yards away as he pointed out individuals circling his apartment.

It was almost surreal to witness dozens of fluttering sillouhuetes come in for a landing, under the moonlight, with the lights of Cairo as a backdrop. He would hold his hand up in the air, and one by one, each pigeon would land on his outstretched finger.

The birds melted into his hands as he coed along with them, stroking them with affection, and relating the stories of each ones accomplishments. We realized immediately his tales of his birds were filled with impossible situations meant to entertain us, and that we were in the presence of a master storyteller.

I must admit, I was not prepared for the in depth education we received over the next three hours as we sat through the entire life history of every bird complete with their baby photos!

Their roost is called a dovecote or loft, and science has declared pigeons to have a sensory center in their brain that allows them to find their home from as far away as 900 miles, the distance most of them can fly nonstop in a 12 hour period.
Racers begin competing as young as six months and can be active up to age ten with an average sporting life of about three years.

They are monitored by computer chips while they fly from as far away as Belgium, back to their Cairo loft in groups that number thousands at a time. Each wears an ankle band coded with their departure time that is monitored along the flight and is noted upon landing so no cheating can take place.

When Avian Flu has prevented him from competing internationally,

Ahmed raced within Egypt, sending his birds as far afield as Aswan and Luxor, covering most of the country. Ahmed told us how he always loses a few birds in every race, some from predators, and others to causes unknown, but also usually gains a few strays that attach themselves to the traveling show along the way, and how they begin their training to fill the gaps as soon as they arrive.

In the course of three hours, I came away almost an expert, inundated in the history of pigeon racing and ready to return home to found my own dovecote.

It was one of those fascinating evenings that come to those who travel off the beaten path, full of wonderful stories and humor one would never be aware of otherwise. I have also rarely known anyone who spoke with such love and commitment to both his animals and their sport. It was not just an education about a particular sport, but also of how the lovely people of Egypt are ready to befriend anyone.

As we were finally ushered out the door, now officially members of the Bahaa family and our heads spinning with pigeon trivia, Ahmed capped off the evening by yelling loud enough for the entire block to hear.

"You should raise pigeons! They will be like your children! And when you are done, you can eat them!"

A SEPARATE REALITY

In Africa, more than anyplace on earth, age commands respect.

As a travel writer who seeks out remote tribal cultures on my own, my white hair has given me entre to societies that are usually closed to tourist groups.

On a continent where 50 is considered old and especially in rural tribes that have no medical facilities and must contend with predatory animals and poisonous snakes as a way of life, I am usually senior in age to most tribal elders or chiefs. My arrival at such places is usually welcomed with an immediate audience with the tribal authority and a crowd of curious people anxious to know how such an ancient dinosaur is wandering around the bush by himself. This fascination has in turn has usually opened the collective memories of ceremony and oral histories that I so dearly love to learn about.

But there have also been times when age has not opened the door and I have been subjected to small tests to prove my worthiness to enter a particular society. Case in point: the Dorje people of Ethiopia.

The Dorje live high in the Guge mountains of central Ethiopia and are known for their tall bee hive shaped thatched huts that resemble the head of an elephant. They are made this way because centuries ago the central mountains of Ethiopia teemed with high altitude elephants that shared the land in harmony with the Dorje, and they build their homes in this manner to this day as an homage to their now extinct neighbors.

I arrived at the village of Chencha unannounced on a Saturday morning to find hundreds of people gathered in a small valley for the weekly market. Such arrivals are usually greeted by a mob of curious children who loudly announce my presence and lead me in. This time was no different. With a child firmly attached to each hand I wandered among the women, seated on the ground with their products showcased on spread blankets, the only outsider present.

Surprised by the general lack of men I could not help but notice that many of the women were puffing away on small homemade pipes that had a clay bowl sitting on top of a bulls' horn. This was not unusual as many tribal women smoke pipes in Africa but I could tell immediately from the aroma that this was not tobacco. They were smoking Khat, a local plant common around the horn of Africa and usually chewed to produce effects similar to marijuana. I did not know at the time that the Dorje prefer to scrape the leaves of these plants for the sticky residue which they sun dry in fist sized blocks that produces enough potency to level a grown man.

I had not seen pipes like this before and wanted to purchase one as a collectable but was let known in no uncertain terms that first I would have to imbibe it with the owner. Now I do not make a habit of such acts nor do I encourage doing so, especially in developing countries where drug laws can get you thrown into a dark pit for the rest of your life, but this was a remote place beyond the hand of the law and I figured one little toke just might give me face to enter their world.

By now I had attracted a large crowd, fascinated by this strange white intruder, all of them urging me on, so with deference to Bill Clinton, I inhaled a tiny bit and a second later felt the top of my head explode. As I did so a murmur of approval spread through the crowd. I had passed the opening round but within a minute I felt as though I was floating above everyone, looking down at them. Apparently I had won them over because several of the women took me by the hand and ushered me into a small dark building where I discovered most of the men.

Seating me on a bench they began to place small glass cruets of amber liquid in front of me that turned out to be home brewed honey wine that they produce from local hives. Since I was already feeling no pain I downed one to the cheers of all present and was given another. Needless to say the number of drinks I consumed was quickly lost in the fog of my mind and the next thing I recall was waking up at night in a hut with several small children urging me to my feet.

I staggered outside to see a large bonfire that seemed to be twirling in circles and realized I was still higher than the surrounding mountains with a sandpaper tongue stuck to the roof of my mouth.

This time my appearance elicited a collective cheer from the gathered crowd who ushered me into their midst where they handed me a drum, and only then did I realize there were people in leopard skins dancing around the fire. I had been accepted. I was now not only part of the tribe but a central figure of the Guge Mountain Musical Drum Ensemble.

I began to beat the drum in cadence with those around me and in my heightened state of awareness merged effortlessly into the soul of the music. Ego vanished as I gave myself to the moment and felt myself connected by an ancient thread that brought these people together through harmonic ceremony. I beat the drum with increasing fervor, creating a rhythm I had not before known myself capable of. Turning to both sides I saw sweaty black faces urging me on, driving me with their own immersion in the music. This was old Africa, the spear and loin cloth Africa that I had hoped still existed, and I was in the middle of it.

I had previously participated in voodoo ceremonies in West Africa and knew that drums were the vehicle used to propel ones consciousness into an altered state. That is the mindset I now pursued.

For a few moments I felt an intuitive knowledge of this ancient way of life, as though I had left my own behind and been born again into theirs, and while I know it was most likely the smoke and drink, a part of me desperately wanted it to be a metaphysical breakthrough, a true path to an altered reality, the kind all true seekers wish for but rarely achieve.

The music was intoxicating, a combination of rhythmic drumming and people chanting a melodic theme over and over while dancers clad in animal skins and carrying spears twirled and jumped over the central fire in a scene that might have been the same when Leo Africanus lived. Dancers rushed at me with raised spears mimicking a hunt from their past while women trilled their tongues in high pitched sonics.

In my mind at least it was the perfect happening where all components came together be they artificially induced or not, but providing me with the kind of unique experience I always hope for.

Sometime in the wee hours the fire and music began to diminish at the same time and one by one the people began to drift away, most of them coming to place a hand on my shoulder in local blessing. I sat there for some time, staring at the star filled night and marveling at not only my acceptance, but inclusion, by these people.

By now I was shivering from the cold and made my way into a surprisingly warm and toasty hut, kept that way by the exhaled breath of the cows and goats that are brought in for the night by the children.

In the morning I was greeted by one and all with the word, "Am Baht", the Amharic word for "father" and spent the day surrounded by eager and happy people sharing their oral histories.
I am not proud for getting high nor am I ashamed of it. I may very well have entered their world without doing so but I simply went with the flow and did what the Dorje wanted me to do.   A traveler should always be aware of being a guest while in another society and both respect and follow their customs. The reader should also consider that what is taboo in one culture may be a way of life for another.

Learning these differences is what travel is all about, and sometimes the rewards far outweigh the cost.

THE 100 YEAR OLD WOMAN

People are pretty much the same the world over but what sets us apart are the minute cultural nuances, the turn of a phrase or interpretation of body language that can take a conversation in a totally new direction, usually with unexpected results.

Irene and I were very excited to have finally made our way to Egypt and our first stop was to see the great pyramids at Giza, directly outside of Cairo. This trip by the way was just a few months before the upheaval that overthrew President Hosni Mubarak.

We arrived quite early before the midday heat and crush of tourists and found ourselves almost alone there except for a large gathering of young school girls who appeared to be on a field trip. We obviously stood out as tourists and within a couple minutes they had surrounded us.

They began peppering Irene with questions, using the opportunity to practice their limited English with a willing participant. We were both quite used to this in our travels, and in fact have come to expect such a reception from people who often wish to practice with a native speaker. I stood back from the crowd so I could hear what they were saying and not interfere.

The girls enunciated their questions with great effort as their use of English was quite limited and they were confining their questions to the standards we always hear such as "Where are you from?" and "Do you like our country?" After my wife identified herself as an American, the questions intensified.

One young lady stood out, jumping up and down yelling, "How old are you?" This of course attracted even more people wondering what all the commotion was about.

My wife gave her age, but the girls' command of English was not sufficient to understand the numerical answer, so Irene began holding up ten fingers at a time to show her age. While doing this she was being bombarded with other questions from these very curious young ladies and kept losing her place trying to keep up with all of them, so she would stop to answer one question, and then go back to holding up her fingers for the first girl who continued to ask how old she was.

This went on for some time when the girl who had inquired about her age finally turned to some of her friends and called out something in what I recognized as Arabic and they all laughed and crowded around.

I asked one of the English speaking girls what she had said and she told me her friend had called her friends to come and meet the American lady who was over 100 years old!

JUNGLE CAPITALISM

Some cultures die because their time has simply come and gone while others are destroyed by those they fascinate. This is a tale of the latter.

Bertrand and I peered through the last row of the millet field, unwilling to give up our only source of cover. The village, a diminutive circle of grass huts, appeared unoccupied, benign, but Bertrand has a vestigial sense about these situations I had come to trust.

Late the previous afternoon we had approached a similar village but the raucous, drunken singing and sporadic gunfire had turned us around. While this village seemed deserted we knew otherwise; it could even be a trap.

We had come to see the Mursi people of Ethiopia's Omo Valley, a heavily armed, violence-prone people who exist as an anomaly among all of Africa's tribal cultures in that their entire existence seems predicated on the single minded, all out aggressive pursuit of money. To learn why, we needed to enter their society.

No sooner did we break cover than we were surrounded by gunmen, hemmed in a tight circle that quickly got smaller until I was staring directly into the barrel of the AK47 that I assumed was held by the village headman.

The Omo Valley is unique in Africa that due to its isolation most anthropologists believe the numerous tribes that dwell within its borders have evolved over the millenniums with no linguistic or stylistic similarities to any other culture on the continent. They have developed within a veritable fish bow. Going a step further, the Mursi seemed to me to be among the most outlandish people I had ever met.

I hired Bertrand, a former foreign legion para and French expatriate in Addis Ababa for his knowledge of the area, its people, and their dialects, but mostly because he is a kindred spirit who makes his living by taking people like me into remote places where forfeiture of life in pursuit of an answer is always possible.

Little is known about the distant origins of the Mursi and they may very well be one of the few African cultures that has not migrated from someplace else but originated in the general area they still occupy, an area some believe to be the original site of the Garden of Eden. There were no roads into the Omo Valley until the mid 1960's and even the Ethiopian government knew little of its denizens who fell under their umbrella of citizenship. Ironically the Mursi owe the debut of their international renown to their women whose big mouths, combined with the Ringling Bros. Barnum and Bailey Circus, put them on the world map.

At puberty, an incision is made beneath the lower lip of a Mursi girl and a wooden insert called a labret, is put in place to stretch the skin. As the lip elongates, larger and larger inserts, handmade from clay, replace the smaller ones, some the size of a small dinner plate. The girl cannot talk or eat while wearing the plate and must remove it to do so.

This practice began a couple hundred years ago when the black kings of Africa were rounding up their own people to sell to white slavers. The prevailing belief at the time was that if the women could be made to look ugly enough, the slavers would pass them by. This did not spare the Mursi from chains, but the practice persisted as a cultural tradition, and today the larger the labret, the more beautiful the woman is considered to be. This also demands a larger dowry of cattle when she is married.

In the 1920's the Ringling Brothers Barnum and Bailey Circus was internationally famous and had agents around the globe, constantly seeking new and interesting acts, especially for their side shows that featured people of unusual size or with deformities, and what could be stranger than the Mursi women with the huge lips?

The circus brought two Mursi women back to New York, putting them into the show and calling them "Ubangis" misusing the name of a river in central Africa and a tribe that dwells within the current borders of Chad. This misnomer was also common in early animated cartoons. The reasons for using that name are unknown. Perhaps the circus scouts had the wrong location on their maps or just wanted an exotic sounding name to sell tickets, but whatever the reason, the Mursi to this day have been stuck with the Ubangi label. They were a huge attraction but died young and left no written or oral record of their life in the modern world, but these unwitting ambassadors opened a flood gate.

In the natural order of events, adventurers, explorers, and curiosity seekers began trickling into the Omo in search of the latest oddity. Foremost among them were Robert Ripley of "believe it or not fame" and early photographers from national Geographic whose photos of the bare breasted women shocked the world but sold piles of magazines. This to me seemed to be the tipping point that sent their culture into a downhill spiral.

While it has long been the norm for indigenous people in developing countries to ask for money in exchange for rights to take their photos, the Mursi embraced this concept with a maniacal zeal that borders on the psychotic. They pursue money with a blind fury for the sake of money itself and no other reason, and Bertrand and I had just placed our lives in the midst of these gun toting uber-capitalists to experience it first-hand.

He had warned me of what to expect; pushing, shoving, threats with a gun, demanding money for their photograph and relentless aggressiveness until we agreed. They swarmed us both, bargaining for a price with finger language and agreement being the nod of a head, then struck ridiculously histrionic poses in their outlandish costumes, designed specifically for the camera. Even after coming to a common number for the photos, they poked, hit, and kicked me, while fighting amongst themselves to be first, and as I raised my camera, always another would jump into the frame at the final second then demand money for essentially ruining the agreed upon shot. It was like being caught in a riot and only the promise of more money to come got them to back off momentarily.

During the brief lull I tried to collect my thoughts. Some of the men had been drinking heavily even though the day was still early. Many of them had a sickly yellow tint to their eyes where white would normally reside. Their costumes were strange amalgamations of whatever cast-off debris they could find from corn cob hats to old torn sports coats, shoes that did not match, and sarongs worn by both men and women. They had swirling white designs on all visible parts of their bodies and most had large ear plugs, besides the various younger women with their pizza plate labrets.

The mere appearance of my camera drove them into a frenzy I would liken to sharks feeding in blood filled waters and I have never before found any

people to be so feral. They are dark skinned even by African standards, most of them the black of ebony, with cracked skin that brings to mind an elephant. Most of their bodies were coated in swirling patterns of a white pigment and layered in the most outlandish costumes. Many coat themselves in animal fat,that after a day in the sun makes them smell overly ripe. There is no symbolic meaning or tribal history for this as can be found in most other tribes. They simply believe the more ridiculous they present themselves the more you will want their photo and that means more money.

Once you take their photo they slide into one of the huts and quickly re-emerge in another equally wild getup, skilled quick change artists, demanding you again take their photo, and to refuse is to invite the spilling of blood.

They would not listen to a blanket offer of money to allow me to roam freely taking photos at will, but insisted on individual payment to each person for each photo, and that quickly passed to one of several roaming women each with intricately woven baskets adorned with porcupine quills, each stuffed with cash, and each woman making change on the spot with the agility of an athlete, their children close by, observing mom while she plied the family business, the next generation in training. Only after doubling my monetary offer did they quit the over the top posing and allowed me to photograph them in more natural settings, but with the men always holding a rifle. They have made this degrading act a science, executed with split second timing and complete tribal cooperation. They operate like a well-oiled machine with the sole purpose of sucking every penny out of every visitor.

My first encounter lasted maybe an hour and left me exhausted and feeling as though I had just gone ten rounds with a superior fighter. We left by their indulgence granted only after the promise of returning the next day with more money, realizing the slightest faux-paux could quickly escalate into violent carnage.

That night we camped in a low thicket, afraid to light a fire in case they had tracked us and agreeing to sleep one at a time to preclude a possible attack. I slept with one eye open feeling safer in the presence of local leopards and poisonous snakes than I did knowing our proximity to the Mursi. It was a sleepless night anyway as I pondered how what had once been a dignified society of hunter gatherers had devolved into a tribal vaudeville act.

We returned early the next day early in hopes of arriving before their daily consumption of home brewed vodka had not yet reached epic proportions and relieved not to hear any gunfire at our approach. After an intense negotiation, Bertrand secured permission for me to enter one of their grass huts which I found to be stifling as a sauna and filled with smoke from a smoldering pit in the center of the room, guarded by a woman clad only in an animal thong, counting money from the stacks piled floor to ceiling all about her. For nomads who travel with little baggage I reckoned it would take a total village effort to carry this mini Fort Knox with them.

Retreating outside into the humid sunlight, the previous days' events repeated themselves with little deviation as they did over the next three days in as many different villages. The Mursi were the purest mercenaries and ultimate capitalists I had ever found and would make even the most hardened Wall Street raider green with envy. This head long, balls out pursuit of money fascinated me and fed my desire to find out what drove such an obsession.

My answer came the following day when Bertrand introduced me to Ogu, a ranger of Mago National Park, the administering power of the Mursi land in the Omo Valley. Ogu had the deep color and tribal scarring of the Mursi and was in fact, one of the very small minority that had forsaken life in the bush for an education and the outer world. Still, quite proud of his heritage, he was more than willing to talk.

I learned that the Mursi are divided into five different groups whose names are of minor importance, and that they cultivate sorghum as a main crop while keeping cattle mostly as a backup during times of drought. These means of income are practiced at the main villages that deter visitors, relegating people like me to see them only in their nomad encampments where each group alternates space according to the needs of the cattle. The women maintain these villages while the men tend to the herds, but all is dropped and they all come running whenever a paying photographer enters their land. Money is now the ultimate pursuit.

According to Ogu, in the beginning the Mursi asked only for a tribute payment for a photo from the occasional trekker intrepid enough to enter their lands. He believes what happened over the following years is mostly due to their inbred, isolated way of thinking, and that is why they believe the more people they asked for money, the more came to pay for their photos, and this, to the Mursi meant they could not only control the white man but take his wealth at the same time, thus imbuing themselves with his power. This seemed a perverted take on the old northwest custom of cannibalizing ones enemies in order to assume their spirit. The Mursi were simply cannibalizing their wallets.

They see the accumulation and hoarding of money as raising their station among the other tribes within the Omo, even if their neighboring cultures do not see it that way, and it does not matter, because to the Mursi their self- perception is all that counts.

They are hugely, materially rich by African standards, but do not live in permanent homes, do not own cars, and certainly do not send their children to schools. When they do part with this self- perceived wealth they use it to purchase weapons and ammunition, easily acquired from over the nearby border from lawless Somalia, or to buy local liquor that for many has become the only nightly ceremony, in order to maintain their own macho view of themselves.

As they have wandered further away from their tribal roots in this pursuit, they have systematically become a self- perpetuating money making machine that has drained any vestige of dignity from their culture.

To many within the Ethiopian government, they are an anachronistic embarrassment and legislation has been enacted to gradually relieve them of their hereditary lands while forcing them into more sedentary lifestyles within the cities. If it comes to that, blood will spill.

In the meantime, they continue to attract visitors and as their bizarre behavior escalates, this observer fears it is only a matter of time before there is a violent encounter that will force the governments hand and sound the final death knell of the Mursi.

A QUICK TRIP TO HELL

In the dead of night on January 12, 2012, nine trekkers were awakened from a sound sleep inside their grass huts on the summit of a remote volcano in northeastern Ethiopia. According to the BBC, they were manhandled outside where five of them; German, Hungarian, and Austrian, were lined up and executed with AK47 Kalashnikov automatic rifles.

Two other people, believed to be from Belgium were seriously injured, while an unidentified third person escaped unharmed. Four additional people were kidnapped, including an Ethiopian policeman, driver, and two German nationals, hustled off into the humid night.

They were all at the Erta Ale volcano in one of the most remote and hostile areas on earth, the Danakil Depression, home of the nomadic Afar people, where temperatures routinely reach 125 degrees Fahrenheit, (49 Celsius.) This was only the latest in a succession of attacks on trekkers to the area, but the first to be credited to the very people who have only recently invited people to enter their land with impunity.

The news chilled my blood because only a couple months prior, I had been asleep in those same huts.

The Afar Revolutionary Democratic Front Militia assumed initial responsibility for this attack, claiming it to be part of their struggle against the Ethiopian government's exploitation of their land and culture. Prior attacks have been blamed on Eritrean bandits, crossing the border to disrupt Ethiopia's burgeoning tourist industry as part of a continuing skirmish that began when the former country succeeded, taking the only national seaport with them.

This attack took place on the summit of Erta Ale, a rarely visited shield volcano whose fiery red backdrop of bubbling gases dancing in the black night must have added a touch of hell to those about to die.

I was a journalist invited by a team of NASA planetary scientists who wished to study the volcano, and make comparisons of it to those of a similar volcano found on Jupiter's moon, IO. My wife, Irene, joined me because she is a true explorer and not one to be left behind no matter how tough the going.

The Afar people are Sunni Muslims who number about 1,500,000 spread throughout Eritrea, Ethiopia, Somalia, and Djibouti. Their history can be traced back at least to the 13TH century when they first appear in the writings of the noted Moroccan historian, Ibn Sa'id.

The great explorer and travel writer Wilfred Thesiger who crossed Afar land in the early 20th century referred to them as a murderous people whose only purpose was killing anyone from another tribe. Little has been written about them since that time because of their extreme isolation and reputation.

They are sometimes referred to as the Danakil as they are closely associated with the great desert of the same name. Theirs' is one of the harshest lifestyles on the planet in one of the most barren regions, and it is this location that thrust them on to the stage of international politics.

As typical nomads, the Afar owe allegiance to no particular country and have had numerous clashes with almost every state they occupy who have tried to impose their way of life upon them. The Afar only recognize the authority of their tribal sultans. Modern nations have usually failed to realize that lines on a map have no meaning to hereditary nomads.

Since the military conflict between Ethiopia and Eritrea ended in 2000, the Ethiopian government has allowed the Afar great autonomy based on this reputation, and they have acted as a natural buffer between the two countries. They have become, knowingly or not, keepers of the no man's land that separates the two countries, and thus the peace, regardless of how tentative. For the most part, this strategy has worked, as there have been relatively few border incidents until recently in an area surrounded by political turmoil and increasing public unrest.

Hand in hand with their reputation as fierce warriors, Afar men, and many young boys, are heavily armed, usually with Chinese made Kalashnikov automatic rifles, easily obtained from across the Red Sea through Yemen or south from Somalia, and many carry hand grenades and a small curved dagger. In contrast to this martial mentality the Afar have a bond with their environment and animals that is beyond the comprehension of most city dwellers. While they do slaughter animals occasionally for meat, it is only after a ceremony asking for the animal's forgiveness and thanking it for providing sustenance. This reverence for wildlife is believed responsible for the preservation of the African Wild Ass, (Equus Africanus) that thrives on their land while now extinct in other areas of Africa it used to populate. To the Afar, the land is their mother, their camels are part of their family, and they will not even step on a plant if they can avoid it. Their connection to the land is absolute because they do not have the distractions of modern life. There is great irony in this when one considers their track record concerning their fellow man.

We met the team in Addis Ababa, the capitol city of Ethiopia, and from there took a flight to Mekele, a small town in the northeast and a city that took heavy shelling from Eritrea in the past. Mekele is the gateway to the Danakil.

In two Land Rovers we headed into the desert for our first stop at the "village" of Berhaile, if a collection of grass huts could be called by that name. Its main attraction is the constant exchange of camel caravans passing through, hauling salt from the sizzling white flats only a few miles away. Along the way we passed numerous burnt out military vehicles and crumbling gun emplacements of volcanic rock that when hit by an artillery shell would themselves become shrapnel. Countless artillery barrages have been exchanged over this valley that separates the sparring nations, and the dogs of war have ravaged the land well. Skeletal cattle and goats sipped stagnant rainwater from old shell craters and foraged on the rare bush.

The salt flats were our first real contact with the Afar as the majority of them eke out a subsistence living by chopping into the thick crust with primitive axes, and using large tree branches as leverage, they pry up enormous slabs of salt weighing hundreds of pounds. This in turn is chopped into small squares and loaded onto the never ending line of camels, both coming and going, under a blistering sun. Night time brings no respite as this operation continues around the clock, day in and day out. This area is known to contain more camels than any other place on earth and they are more valued than some peoples' lives.

It is scene straight out of the Bible and is little changed since the time of Christ, and yet, some of these desert wanderers have decided there are

more profitable and less strenuous ways to make a living, so they have recently joined the entrepreneurial ranks of the eco- tourism business.
A small number of Afar have begun contracting to guide groups of pilgrims to the Erta Ale, a torturous trek of several miles over razor sharp volcanic rock that can shred a hikers boots in less than an hour. To stumble or fall is to invite major lacerations. There is no trail per se, only meandering flat spots between boulders the size of cars, that rises a mere 600 feet above the valley floor and must be negotiated at night as it is simply too hot during daylight hours. It is extreme trekking at its best, and only the hardiest would attempt this journey.

We argued over a price to enter their land at their minimalist village at Dodom, miles from the volcanoes' base, where several men armed with automatic rifles stood in the shadows as we nervously handed over our money. In exchange, we were promised a gunman to accompany each of us into the wasteland, and to bring us back safely.

We had to ignore countless stories of Afar atrocities and accept what others had told us about their loyalty once they have given their word. They themselves told us about bandits in the area who would leave us alone while under their protection. At that time I had not yet heard anything about the Afar Revolutionary Democratic Front Militia and they had not surfaced on international radar.

Dodom is the gateway to Erta Ale, and from there we crossed a desolate moonscape of black rock that rivaled a scene from Mordor. We were told that the Afar would bring food and water, but to them that meant a stale biscuit and half a liter of water each. While the sun sank behind us the temperature remained the same, and the earth trembled under our feet, constantly reminding us that we were trespassing on a living, churning, cauldron of magma. My headlamp proved mostly ineffective, only providing distorted shadows that danced among the looming boulders, turning them into wraiths reaching out to haul us into the underworld. I fell into step behind the black silhouette of the gunman leading me, who spoke no English and seemed at best to tolerate my presence.

Our small party was soon spread over several miles, each of us making his or her own way with little assistance from the Afar other than to squat on top of a neighboring boulder and wait for us to catch up. I could not halt the thought of what would happen if this gunman actually had to defend

me. Would he fire at a local person? Would I be his victim? From here on out we were at their mercy.

Irene had gone ahead, riding a camel because she has only one good eye, and we agreed she would not be able to negotiate this ascent even under the best of conditions on foot. Within minutes of our departure, she was out of my sight and I had to trust that I would find her safe when I reached the summit.

Six hours later I collapsed with bloody hands and feet, totally spent from exertion and the rising heat as we neared the crest. Realizing I am a bit long in the tooth for such expeditions I wondered if I had bit off more than I could chew for what I considered to be my capstone adventure after 30 plus years of remote exploration. From where I fell, I could see an eerie red glow as though Lucifer were beckoning me. I was almost at the volcanoes' summit but could go no further. I was dehydrated and had no food all day.

I lay on the ground, gasping for air and worrying about my wife when I noticed a silhouette approaching from above. Not knowing if it was a bandit, my "security" guard, or an apparition induced by my condition, I only remember looking up at the countless stars overhead and thinking how beautiful a place it was.

Isn't it strange what enters the human mind when confronted with death or the unknown?

I had always said that when my time comes to depart the earth, I would like it to happen while on an expedition, doing what I love rather than lying in a hospital bed hooked up to tubes. As the black hulk loomed over me I could discern a rifle leveled at me and flashed on the old Indian saying, "It is always a good day to die."

The ghost flicked on my headlamp, peered into my face and grunted. It was my assigned gunman whom I had not seen for over two hours. He had returned to see what had happened to me, and I was so disoriented at the moment I did not know if he was going to rob me or kill me. What he did was kneel down, roll himself in his long robe, and curl up to sleep beside me. I suppose he thought I was going to spend the night were I was. In seconds he was snoring like a buzz saw and as my mind slowly cleared, it was all I could do to keep from laughing at the absurdity of the situation.

This man who could easily kill me with impunity and disappear into the night, had come back to honor his commitment, and suddenly, there we were, laying on the side of a trembling volcano together, under a glittering sky that under different circumstances would have been a glorious sight. I believe it will be one of those bizarre moments that flash back at the moment of my real death.

In a few minutes I staggered to my feet, waking him, and together we crested the summit, staring into a bloody red and yellow stew of churning molten lava that every few seconds sent a gas bubble shooting several yards into the sky, exploding like fireworks. The heat was intense and I could only stare in awe for a few seconds before retreating.

I vaguely remember stumbling into a grass hut with Irene standing over me. She had arrived hours ago and had this stupendous light show all to herself, secure in the knowledge that my experience and good sense had only shortly delayed me along the trail. I pulled her into my arms and fell asleep too tired to find the rest of our group, wondering if they were getting the data they came to find.

It seemed to be only a few seconds later when I was prodded awake by a rifle barrel and saw the first cracks of dawn breaking. Four hours had passed. The Afar were telling us we needed to begin our descent before the sun rose higher as it was already like the inside of an oven.

There was no food or water, but everyone was assembled, and being urged to shoulder our packs quickly. We had no time to discuss the evenings' events as a group because our gunman was emphatically urging us downward with his rifle. I surveyed the distance over the barren moonscape at my feet, thinking I had never been in such an isolated place as this brown, forbidding, glorious land, as far as I could see. I could not make out where we had come from the previous day. I only knew it would be a torturous journey of many miles to get back.

I was just getting Irene on her camel when two quick shots rang out and the high pitched whine of a bullet passing our heads sent us scurrying behind a large boulder. One more shot rang out and I was not about to look and see where it was coming from. Irene had taken a bad fall during this confusion, thinking she had sprained her ankle and could not stand, so we wrapped it tight with duct tape. All I could think was that our Afar had betrayed us, when suddenly our personal gunman motioned for us to get going downhill, and he stood there with his rifle leveled at the summit as though providing us cover. We moved fast as we could travel, Irene's camel breaking into a downhill trot that had her holding on for dear life, while I practically ran, praying that she would not take a bullet.

There was no more shooting and our gunman caught up with us within a mile. We could not communicate enough to ask what had happened but he seemed to take it in stride as if it were all part of the trip. I was beginning to think they had simply fired over our heads to provide a touch of drama, but will never know. Irene's camel trotted off into the distance while I staggered over the unforgiving land, caring only that she get back safely.

Five hours later I reached our camp and collapsed into her arms, curling up into a fetal position, my entire body cramping from a total expenditure of electrolytes. We had gone all this time without food and only a liter of water. Ken forced a package of dry Gatorade down my throat that brought me back from the brink in a few minutes, and was helping me to the Land Rover when the Afar surrounded us demanding additional money.

I recall a lot of yelling as our driver gunned the engine and we sped away, showering everyone with sand, and listening for the crack of a bullet coming at us. We did not stop until many miles away and then only to look at each other in silence, trying to comprehend what we had just gone through.

Two months later, while watching a BBC broadcast about this latest attack, I received an e-mail saying that our driver, Berhanu, and guide, Ghet, may have been with the group that were the target. Several days later the BBC announced the release of the two kidnapped hostages with no explanation other than the attackers had apologized to them. There is still no word about the murdered people or what is being done to find their killers. My wife and I could have been the ones who spent our final moments staring into a rifle barrel at the lip of hell.

Since watching that broadcast I have replayed our experience over and over. I am convinced that the Afar we dealt with had honored their part of the bargain and remember my personal guard taking a defensive stance while Irene and I retreated.

I believe the Afar Revolutionary Democratic Front Militia to be a small minority of this culture, as exists in all cultures, and that the majority of the Afar are honorable people in their own way. They need much work on their social skills if they are to deal with foreign visitors, however I think this latest violence will prevent them from having many clients in the near future. They are a people in major transition, trying to enter the modern world while clinging to the old ways.

Two weeks after returning home we discovered that Irene's twisted ankle was actually a fractured fibula and the reason I had collapsed on the volcano was because I had multiple blood clots in both legs and lungs and never should have made it out of there alive.

Today we are both grateful for the experience and the memories, but have decided that our next journey will be a river cruise.

DANCING IN THE DESERT WITH BOB MARLEY

After coming off the Erta Ale Volcano Irene did not know that her sprained ankle was a broken leg and I did not know I was extremely ill, thinking it was simple exhaustion, so together we decided to reach one more destination before returning to the real world.

With her duct taped leg she insisted that she was good to go, never for a second thinking something as minor as a sprained ankle should postpone an adventure. So we took off for one of the more colorful and unique settings in all of Africa, a series of mineral lakes full of bubbling sulfur geysers, a gorgeous natural phenomenon of emerald green and brown water surrounded by yellow and gold rock formations that looked like they were made for a movie set.

We were near the border of Eritrea, in a vast open desert, so there was a heavy presence by the Ethiopian army there acting as a security force for the small number of travelers that enter the area. They gave us a friendly greeting and pointed out the trail head to me. It was immediately obvious that Irene could not make it in her present condition as the lakes sat on a plateau with a rather sheer rise full of unstable shale that had to be negotiated to reach the top. The Ethiopian soldiers assured us they were there to provide for the safety of their visitors and that she was in good hands. I had no reason to doubt them so she elected to stay with our vehicle while I went on to photograph the lakes.

The soldiers were a great relief to me. I only required a couple hours to take the photos I needed, and when I left, Irene was bouncing around in her seat, listening to tunes on her I-pod, so I knew all was well. I took a final look back after cresting the hill thinking about the irony of having high quality music available in one of the most ancient and barren deserts on earth.

I got amazing photos of a surreal landscape unlike anything I had seen any place on earth, filled with golden ochre and yellow hills, bubbling pools of gas churning the waters, and covered by a cerulean sky without a cloud in sight, all a result of the heavy mineral deposits that abound in this highly volcanic area. All it needed to complete the picture were a couple of dinosaurs. Surreal shaped fingers of rock probed for the sky like giant hands and an overpowering sulphur cloud filled the air causing me to pull my kufeya from my neck and wrap it around my face, and still my eyes were tearing up from the vapor cloud. The mass of colors were beyond description and made me think that God was painting there. It was a landscape from another planet.

With my shots in the can I crested the hill on my way back and saw more soldiers than I remembered surrounding our vehicle all waving their rifles in the air, and thinking the worst had happened, I took off at a dead run to get back to Irene.

It seems that while I was gone a couple soldiers saw her bouncing around in the vehicle and went over to make sure she was all right. They had never seen or heard of an I-pod and so she handed each of them an ear piece.

She just happened to be listening to a Bob Marley song at the time, and Marley, all these years after his death, remains a hero throughout much of Africa, especially in Ethiopia.

When the startled soldier heard "I Shot the Sherriff" coming out of this tiny little machine in the middle of a barren desert his eyes widened and he yelled, "It's Bob! You know Bob" and promptly called all of his buddies over to listen. They were mesmerized and had never seen anything like this tiny, wonderful machine, let alone heard music of this quality before. In a few minutes word had gone out on their radios and more jeeps full of troops were on the way.

When I reached the vehicle, out of breath and worried to death, I found Irene surrounded by a dozen green clad soldiers all dancing with their rifles to Bob Marley and passing the earphones around.

JUMPING INTO MATRIMONY

The bridegroom stands naked, stripped except for a ceremonial sash announcing his transition from boyhood to man.

He is weak as he has not eaten for days and he has been alone in the forest praying and fasting

He will take a running start to jump onto the backs of six live bulls. If he falls he will be beaten within an inch of his life by the women of his tribe, but if he succeeds in traversing this living walkway, he will be married.

Welcome to a Hamer Bull Jumping Ceremony, one of the most incredible rites of ceremonial passage in all of Africa.

When cultures evolve inside a fish bowl a byproduct is often ceremonies and rituals virtually incomprehensible to the outside world that are unexplainable in logical terms. The Omo Valley of Southern Ethiopia is such a fishbowl, and the tribes that call it home have no linguistic or stylistic linkage to any other cultures on the African continent. It is so isolated that some anthropologists offer the theory that it once held the Garden of Eden. The earliest evidence of man comes from nearby Olduvai Gorge.

The Omo Valley first became a blip on the public consciousness in the 1930's when the Ringling Bros. Barnum and Bailey Circus brought two Mursi tribal women to New York to put them on display in their "freak show" with their oversized plate like lip labrets, but public curiosity died young as did the two displaced ladies. Today, at least by western standards, equally bizarre rituals are numerous in the Omo.

The Bull Jump ceremony lasts several days with local people being summoned from all over the valley by small brass trumpets that the young women blow from dawn to dusk, before, during, and after the ceremony itself. The girls are supervised by a female shaman, a woman identified by her tall ostrich feather and who wields immense power within the tribe. Because it is a wedding, everyone dresses their best. The women coat their hair with red ochre that under the mid- day sun melts until they are a beautiful earth tone from head to foot. Their hand stitched cowhide loin cloths and layers of glorious beadwork are a hallmark of bush handiwork and fashion. For the men, painted faces, hair feathers, and a shoulder slung AK47 are the order of the day.

The ceremony begins in earnest when tribesmen from a separate clan than that of the groom arrive with their long switches of flexible tree branches. The women of the groom's family will taunt them with the most disgusting insults possible, degrading not only their manhood but their families until the men begin to lash out at the bare backed women, scourging them into bloody pulps. If a women cries out she will be ostracized, but this never happens. In fact they return over and over for more silent suffering, saying that it is how they prove their love for their tribe.

This scourging becomes, in effect, their social security blanket because Hamer women long outlast their men and are not allowed to re-marry. If a widowed Hamer lady bears a much scarred back she will be tenderly cared for in her old age by the entire tribe, but if she is unscarred, her existence will be minimal and hard.

When the scourging is over the entire clan that has been gathering all day, retreats to an isolated part of the forest where the brides' family has brought their cattle herd for the groom's inspection. The groom will carefully choose six bulls for the ceremony whose backs he will be required to run across. The women dance, sing, and noisily blow their bugles while the groom selects his cattle, looking for calm bulls that ignore the noise and will not move while he is on top of them.

When he has made his choice, his aides, called, Maza, all married Hamer men who have successfully run the bulls, will push the hapless creatures together, holding both their horns and tails in an effort to calm the totally spooked animals.

The groom will get a running start, jump onto the back of the first bull, run across all six backs and jump down to the ground; then he will turn and repeat this maneuver three separate times. Should he fall or even hesitate for a moment, the women of the tribe will beat him with sticks until he is unconscious. When he comes to he will be shunned and must retreat into the forest for prayer and contemplation. In one year he may attempt the ceremony once again.

If he should succeed in crossing all six of the bulls, three times each without falling, he is married and in great favor with all. Only at this time will he be taken to his bride's village to meet her for the first time as the parents of both bride and groom have arranged the entire wedding in secret. The groom will pay the brides' father a dowry of several cattle and a firearm, preferably an AK47 for the privilege of taking a wife.

As bizarre as some of these ceremonies may seem to western readers, I cannot help but wonder what remote tribal people would think of our ways should they ever have the means to experience them.

How would a remote villager perceive a ballet or an opera? With their long traditions of oral storytelling I believe they would embrace live theater. They would most likely be stunned by aquariums that allow them to see living creatures underwater but appalled or even sickened by zoos that enslave other creatures in enclosures. Our religious ceremonies are not that dissimilar, and in fact many animist societies would recognize much of the physical trappings of western style Christianity.

A mere decade ago many remote cultures would have been shocked by any image on an electronic screen but with the recent infusion of trekkers into these areas, cellphones and digital cameras have become ubiquitous while satellite dishes proliferate on top of mud houses and canvas yurts.

What seems bizarre to one person is daily life to another.

When I look at reality television I think a Hamer bull jump is rather tame stuff in comparison.

LAST OF THE BUSHMEN

An enraged baboon is a terrifying sight, especially when it's right in front of you.
It crashed out of the bush no more than twenty feet from me, shrieking and baring its two inch fangs.

I had just gone from pursuer to prey and stood frozen in place at this turn of events when the dull thud of an arrow entered its' neck and the creature tumbled over, convulsing as the poison did its job.

Turning to see the Hadzabe smiling broadly as he knocked another arrow into his bow, I realized I was now in the Stone Age.

The Hadza Bushmen of western Tanzania are a dying race, isolated from the rest of Africa by language, culture, and an absolute refusal to update an ancient way of living. They travel light, with minimal possessions, sleeping in caves or on the ground in overnight grass shelters, as feral as the land itself. Monkey and baboon are their main diet with an occasional Kudo or gazelle unfortunate enough to come within range of their bows whose arrow tips carry a potent neurotoxin. They often shoot from the hip while on the run, and rarely miss.

They have no chiefs and the women have an equal say in tribal affairs.
They move easily about every two weeks, and if a large animal is killed in a hunt, the entire clan will relocate to it rather than bring the animal back with them. They live entirely off the land, as the most skilled of hunters and with an encyclopedic knowledge of the flora and fauna that is both nourishment and medicine to them.
These bushmasters are a true window into mankind's own past; living examples of how we outlasted the dinosaurs, and proof that even minimal technology is not desired by everyone. They are our own living ancestors.

My entre to their world came at the end of an all- night thunderstorm that swept over the Ngorogoro highlands like the wrath of God, churning the rocky forest into a quagmire that sucked my land Cruiser to a halt three separate times. Julius finally parked us under an enormous Baobab to slog his way into the Bushmens' camp and announce my coming.

The Baobab was slick, rubbed shiny with the fat and entrails of hundreds of kills. Countless skulls and horn racks were hung from it, a living testimony to the hunter's prowess and receptacle of the local clans' essence. The tree was the tribes' ju ju and each night they hung their bows from it to have them absorb the power of their killed prey. It was a bizarre place to wait, a primeval scene in the morning fog, a six thousand year old photo of ritual, ceremony, and esoteric belief.

Julius whistled from the top of a rise and as I crested the muddy hill, there, huddled under a rock outcropping, around a tiny fire, were the hunched figures of the Bushmen. They squatted on their haunches, clothed in rags and baboon hides, their sing song tongue echoing off the interior rock face added a surreal quality to the moment. I was looking at first man, unchanged and unaltered by time or events.

They ignored my approach and as the smoke from their fire reached my nose a second, more familiar aroma was mingled with it when I noticed them passing a pipe that appeared to have been carved from an animal horn. Without introduction, a wiry young man with a halo of baboon fur around his head stood up, turned, and handed me the pipe. Now all eyes were on me and knowing this to be a defining moment I inhaled deeply. Fighting the urge to cough I held the smoke and felt its probing fingers enter my brain, numbing my senses. This was not a random act. For many tribes like the Hadza, entrance to an altered state is both ritual and ceremony and in this case it was preparation for a hunt.

Smoking with them gave me the necessary face as all six of them rose at this point to pound me on the back, laughing. This threw me completely off guard. Julius had told me they were friendly people who are known for embracing the occasional stranger but I was not prepared to be handed a bow with arrows that appeared razor sharp or prodded to follow them down the rise and into the bush.
Puzzled by their metal weaponry, I would later learn that these minimalist hunters trade animal skins and meat with the neighboring Baigara tribe; nomads and expert blacksmiths, who trade their metal arrow tips and spear heads in a unique symbiotic relationship.

The bow was almost as tall as me and strung with animal tendon. My host motioned towards a tree; another test that could lead me deeper into their world. The bow pull was incredibly hard and my arm shook in the effort to draw it sufficiently. My first two arrows were true but short. When I imbedded the third one in the tree there was a mutual cry of approval and everyone motioned for me to follow.

Within seconds I was alone in the bush as they moved like leopards, disappearing into the shadows. I followed their tracks easily in the mud but they themselves were silent and every few minutes one would return to make sure I was still alive, then wheel and stalk off, hunched in a crouch, arrow on the bowstring, ready to fire.

It was then that the baboon lunged and was instantly cut down before I could react.
The baboon was returned to the cave, carried piggyback like a sleeping child and almost as large as the man who shot it. Two Hadza sliced a hunk of bark from the highly flammable Commiphora tree and quickly made a friction fire using two sticks and their bush knife. Within minutes the animal was skinned and the meat placed directly on the open fire to sear. One hunter approached me and spread the animal's blood across my face in symbolic acknowledgement of my participation. The hide would become a tunic or carry bag and the skull would soon hang from the juju tree, its essence adding to the power and prestige of the clan. The heart and liver were passed about and eaten raw but I managed to beg off on this delicacy.

As the meat cooked I wandered down the hill, looking into their makeshift huts and photographed the giggling women who found me amusing. One bright eyed baby smiled before returning to its mother's breast. I was overwhelmed by the images, information, and instant immersion that hit like a plunge into ice water that I was in the eye of an entire culture most of the world will never know existed. Within an hour of our meeting I had smoked with the clan, shot their arrows, and participated in a hunt; the immensity of this traveler's gift was almost overwhelming.

I returned to the fire and sat in the dirt, part of the circle of hunter/gatherers, chewing stringy hunks of sizzling baboon, and though we had no common language, I was at that moment, one of them.

As the sun sank behind the shadow of Ngorogoro Crater, turning the Great Rift wall a deep purple, the Hadza talked on into the night, telling stories and relating oral histories. These people who have never known electricity or plumbing or even a roof over their heads are happy and content and made me think long and hard about my own life choices. In the end I could not say if I felt my own existence to be better or worse than theirs, but am fortunate to have had the experience of comparison.

Later, under a full moon, Julius interpreted much of the Hadza creation myth that entails three separate epics, all of which portray them as the first people to populate the earth. In all of them, placed centuries ago, life is the same as it is today. Surprisingly, a 2003 DNA study conducted by Stanford University declared the Hadza to be one of three primary genetic divisions from which all of mankind has descended. Their physical location, only a few kilometers from Olduvai Gorge, where some of the earliest archeological proof of first man has been uncovered, gives credence to this theory.

Today the Hadza are believed to number less than 3,000 and of these maybe only 2-300 still live totally as subsistence hunter/gatherers. The Tanzanian government has offered subsidized housing and formal education but mostly it has been refused.

Since 1964 the policy of Tanzania has been to attempt assimilation of cultures like the Hadza that have been officially declared, "embarrassing" for perpetuating their traditional lifestyle. Government pressure to "modernize" is intense as Tanzania joins a long list of countries that have obliterated their own cultural heritage.

The history of white contact has traditionally been the downfall of indigenous cultures, so it is rather ironic that this current mind set in East Africa is all home grown.

TALES FROM ELSEWHERE

THE SHAMAN OF SAN REGIS

The clouds in the Amazon were the biggest surprise, towering edifices of mashed potatoes that when backlit by the sinking golden sun seemed to glow from within like alabaster night lamps. Most formations were vertical, standing like sentinels over the jungle canopy, scraping the underbelly of heaven.

It was during such a sunset that Uciel guided our skiff ashore to a milling crowd of excited children.

The village of San Regis is a flyspeck on Perus' Amazon River that receives few outside visitors, and even fewer come to seek out the Shaman, Corola. As travelers who consider life to be a quest, my wife and I have sought out holy men, brujos, shaman, soothsayers, and all manner of spiritual guides the world over; now we were deep in the jungle once again, this time to find a lady who has spawned myths.
Carola is known far and wide in the rain forest, a young mother of two with a third on the way, leading a normal village life with her wood carver husband, while at the same time acting as spiritual caretaker and healer to literally hundreds of jungle dwellers spread over many roadless miles. Her prestige and position are beyond reproach. The role of shaman is often misunderstood in the west, associated with black magic, spells and the use of drugs. While these things all have their place, the actual practitioners are as varied as in any profession. Carola is known as a "White" shaman, a healer and spiritual guide.

To be a shaman is a life long journey, passed from elder to youth, requiring years of intense learning and dedication, usually, but not always, commencing in childhood when the spirits determine the next candidate. Few can stay the course as the long years require a strict diet, sexual abstinence, and unquestioning obedience to the master's regime that requires vast knowledge of the natural world including the preparation and ingestion of psychotropic plants.

Uciel, born and raised in the jungle, was a contemporary of Corola, who had watched many fail in this quest as she continued to advance her metaphysical education, growing closer and closer to the spirit world until she occupied a separate reality. As he guided us down the river, he shared his own stories in a matter of fact manner.

After four years of shamanistic study, Uciel's friend was ordered to kill his dog as a sign of loyalty to his teacher, and so he did. Three more years of training passed and again he was ordered to kill his latest dog which he did without hesitation. In his eighth year he was ordered to kill his daughter and refused, terminating his training with great loss of face in his village. That woman was Uciels' wife and the apprentice shaman was her father. Uciel told us he did not know if the shaman would have allowed his father in law to carry out the execution or if it was all a test, but either way, the outcome would have been accepted by all involved. His father in law eventually took his own life, unable to live with his shame. Neither Uciel nor his wife holds the shaman responsible. Such is their culture.

Another story recounted a dark tale that apparently is common place in which the shaman carves a chunk from a kapok tree and inserts a personal item from a person they wish to kill. The kapok is a fast, self- healing tree, and within weeks, new growth covers the removed area, imprisoning the enclosed item, during which time the intended victim slowly suffocates to death as though being strangled by the tree itself. But in the jungle where lives are dominated by myth and legend and the spirit world is the same as the waking world, who is to say what is truth or fiction?

To Uciel, both worlds are concurrent but he reiterated time and again that Carola was a 'white" shaman, meaning she only used her powers for good. When I asked if a white shaman could perform evil deeds he looked at me as though I were crazy. In shamanism as in all of life, there is a ying and yang that never meet.

Uciel had brought a catfish as offering and as we landed, inquired of the village headman if Corola might see us, and we were not surprised to hear that she was already waiting for us at her "temple" in the forest.

We followed the trail away from the village to a thatched roof palapa where a hunched figure sat in deep shadow. Entering silently my wife and I both felt a palpable yet indescribable presence. We sat on a low wooden bench as Corola looked up with deep black eyes that told me she was returning from another place. She was small except for her baby bump, with raven hair cascading down like flowing water. Uciel spoke to her in Spanish and she answered in her native Kukama Kukamiria, a dying tongue once used universally throughout this river basin before white contact, then quickly switched to Spanish. Her voice was soft and flowing with a soothing quality of assurance. She greeted us as pilgrims and said had we been tourists she would not have met with us, then proceeded to pass around a bottle of ayahuasca, the hallucinogenic beverage distilled from indigenous plants that is used as a vehicle to visions within the spirit world. It was not for our consumption, only offered as information; indeed, without training, it might have killed us; but its odor alone revealed its power.

She spoke of her early training that came from her grandfather whose wooden likeness stared at us from a mask on the wall and she allowed us to question her for some time but her answers seemed to emanate from a source outside of her. She spoke of the need to enter the other world in order to access the power to heal and how the granting of such power by the spirits was due to the purity of her own life. She spoke of the "essence" of the jungle present in all things, living and inanimate, that I would equate to the belief in a soul, but when I inquired as to the extent of her powers her voice suddenly became masculine and told me that was an area left unspoken. I was surprised how forthcoming she was but she said it was because she had "seen" us and knew us to be seekers of truth.

She went on to tell us of numerous people she had healed, including those with broken bones and snake bites, and I had no cause to doubt her claims. In a land without medical doctors the power of belief is supreme, and in fact, most of the medicines of my own western world originated in this very same rain forest. How ironic that the modern world is slowly destroying this ancient pharmacy by over logging and clear cutting to build cities for more people while destroying the medicines to keep them alive.

At the time I had many questions but remember none of them now. I only remember being mesmerized by her eyes as though she had insight to my very being and I felt with absolute certainty that I would meet her again. Since then I have wondered if she had altered my personal memory in some unknown way.

Our visit ended with her rolling an enormous spliff of tobacco dipped in ayahuasca and passing the smoke over us in a purification ceremony. I left with a wooden mask carved by her husband, the face of a shaman in the spirit world inlaid with coca seeds, the dominate indigenous plant that is the source of most potions. As we walked down the trail I looked back and Corola was already in another place.

In the western world most of us rely on modern medicine to perpetuate our lives and that medical world for the most part dismisses people like Carola, but we tend to forget that long ago it was the shamans who first introduced their ways to the outside world, and that was the beginning of the evolution of that very same modern medicine we rely on today. But unlike western medical doctors, the shaman also tends to the soul.

About a month after returning home I had a vivid dream in which Corola simply smiled at me and then disappeared and I awoke feeling better than I had in a very long time. Then I wondered if it was a dream or real, but it did not matter.

In the world of shamans, all realities are the same.

PERUVIAN TROUT

After a wonderfully exhausting day exploring the ruins of Macchu Picchu in Peru, Irene and I were ready for a large dinner.

We wandered into the tiny dining room of the only restaurant in the village of Agua Caliente at the base of the cliffs to find it jammed with hungry trekkers and an ear shattering noise level.

We had to yell to be heard over the roar of the Urubamba River, raging directly outside the window and the excited conversations of all the people just back from a day on the heights of the famous Incan hideout.

The Urubamba is known for its delicious fish, especially the trout, so Irene and I both ordered this local delicacy.

The waiter returned in a minute to apologize, saying they only had one trout left, so I let Irene have that one while I ordered chicken.

Waiting for our dinners, I saw an elderly white haired man wading out into the swirling current of the river, making his way from one boulder to the next, obviously with great difficulty. After fighting his way to the middle he squatted down with the waters crashing over him and I caught a glimpse of him holding onto a boulder looking like he was about to be swept away by the surge. Occasionally he stood up and appeared to be struggling to keep his balance.

I was getting angry that no one was helping this older man cross the river and about to call the waiter over to alert him to the situation when I saw another waiter outside yelling back and forth with him. The old man fought his way ashore and handed the waiter a basket.

A second later the first waiter returned to tell us that they now had another trout.

THE CURANDEROS OF LIMA

Sometimes the power of belief is the most important part of a medical treatment.

At the witches market in Lima, Peru, the curanderos gather in early morning, setting up their stalls and hanging their banners. Crowds are already there to see them. Curandero is their preferred name but some people call them shamans, and in this part of the world they are both spiritual advisors and medical healers.

Most of them are women but gender is not a requirement, dressed in traditional garb; bowler hats with layered petticoats, most chewing a wad of cocoa leaves. Each stall holds a colorful banner proclaiming the woman's specialty, and all have cell phone numbers and website addresses because this most ancient mode of healing is slowly using technology to advertise while keeping both feet in the old world.

Each stall is an extension of its owner/practitioner, offering talismans, potions, and religious icons to the faithful. There are magnets to draw an evil spirit from a body and special paper money to bribe them when they refuse. Animal parts and ground herbs are for sale with detailed listings of their healing properties and instructions for their use. Over the silence of respect, whispered prayers and private incantations can be heard. Then there are the guinea pigs.

At the stall of Dona Yessy who has come all the way from Bolivia, incense is burning on an impromptu altar next to prepackaged love potions and a guidebook of how to place a spell on someone in Spanish. Her banner states, "Diagnostica con cuy" meaning she uses a guinea pig to tell her what ails her patients.

In Peru, guinea pig is a dining delicacy featured on almost every restaurant menu, but these furry little creatures are also an integral part of the curanderos' repertoire and the spiritual legacy of the country.

The patient lies prone while la Dona passes the tiny pig over her body, up and down and all around, bringing to mind a sort of rodent CAT scan. The tiny pigs, seeming to know their role, sniff the air as if scenting the patient's ailment. Then, holding the pig next to her ear, la Dona's face goes through a myriad of contortions as she listens to what the critter has supposedly found because theatrics are important to establish the mood. Once the pig has diagnosed the patient's malady, Dona Yessy will know if she has to place an egg under the table, beneath the patient's heart or bring in the big gun, an armadillo, whose body oils will be used to combat the ailment. In worst cases a senior shaman may have to be called in to begin entreating the power of cocoa leaves, not only a natural remedy, but a vehicle to the spirit world for several millenniums.

While all this may sound unbelievably naïve to some readers, is it really that farfetched?

Most modern medicines in industrialized nations had their origins in the rain forests of South America and were introduced to the outside world through white contact with traditional healers, shaman, and medicine men who were on intimate terms with herbal remedies and indigenous plants that held healing properties. For many people in rural areas, this is the only form of medicine they have ever had access to. In large cities like Lima, it is not unusual to find a curandero operating from a store front next door to a modern hospital with patients lined up at both.

At the witches market there was none of the hangdog look you find in the waiting rooms of modern hospitals. The people waiting there were happy and upbeat, talking animatedly as in a party atmosphere because they all believe they will be cured. For these people, faith is the most important medicine.

Just as in western medicine, ongoing education is necessary. A curandero never stops learning, reading, investigating new potions and remedies, because as in all forms of shamanism, being a curandero is a lifelong commitment to helping mankind.

Before leaving, I ask Dona Yessy how the guinea pig speaks to her and she gives me an enigmatic smile, saying, "You will have to ask the pig." He stares at me with large unblinking eyes, saying nothing. Of course the pig does not speak to me. I have neither the wisdom nor the training to communicate with it but have seen too much to dispute it. In either case, that is unimportant. In this place, faith is all that matters.

In this land where spiritualism goes hand in hand with modern technology, being called a witch is a very high compliment.

AN OLD WORLD MASTER

In the mountainous interior of Greece, near Meteoras, gigantic granite fingers, most of them topped with Christian monasteries, point skyward like supplicant fingers tipped with prayers.

They are a stone's throw from the pass of Thermopylae where in 480 B.C. 300 Spartans defined their name in a last stand versus 10,000 Persian mercenaries, and local life has changed little since those ancient halcyon days. Monks reach their near vertical cells in hand cranked cable cars and pull up fresh bread and locally caught fish in baskets on long ropes. Rock climbers on shear faces might be startled by a friendly hermit offering them a rest several hundred feet above the earth in this land where the old world collides with the new.

It was there that my wife and I, on the advice of a friend, began a search. I had heard a story about an orthodox priest who had forsaken the outer world to pursue a life of quiet contemplation fueled by art rather than prayer, or rather, to his way of thinking, art that was prayer. I had been told he painted like Raphael and that those who knew him shielded him from outside influences allowing him complete immersion in his personal form of worship. This was the kind of story we travel to find but realized our chances of finding such a man, if he even existed, were minimal; still, we have always felt the journey to be more relevant than the destination, and so, our numerous inquiries went unanswered until we met George the taxi driver.

Like most Greeks, George spoke excellent English, accented from his years as an expatriate in New York, and who caught us completely off guard by answering our by now redundant questions by saying, "You mean father Pefkis!" and he proceeded to endow the fable with new and fascinating information.

According to George, the good father was a very holy man who worshipped God through his work, creating only religious icons that he considered to be prayer carriers, a direct line to the Almighty if you will. He also told us the priest had qualities that could not be explained by rational means, and added, "You will find out. He will know before you arrive whether you are seekers or tourists."

That is why I began to wonder if we were victims of a hoax when the next day, after a very long drive, he deposited us at a rickety looking auto mechanic's shop next to a roadside diner and motioned for us to climb the stairs. The stairwell was so dark the single bare bulb stole our night vision until I pushed the door at the top open and was assaulted by a kaleidoscope of color. It was a painting atelier the likes of which we had never encountered that quickly overloaded the senses.

The walls were thickly hung with icons, traditional religious scenes painted on wooden panels with gold leaf backgrounds and static people isolated as the subject matter. There were hundreds of them and many more on easels in various states of progress. Most importantly, in that dimly lit room, the paintings seemed to carry a life of their own, glowing from within. Whether one knows art or not it provides a gut feeling when in the presence of greatness, like entering the Louvre Galleries or a main salon of the Prado, and here, in a rickety attic over an auto repair shop, was an equal. My immediate thought was that we had entered a poor man's Sistine Chapel.

While still trying to process what we were witnessing I sensed more than heard a presence and turned to meet this master artist. If our unannounced presence offended him it was not apparent as he stepped forward extending a hand and as I took it a sensation washed over me that I was directly connected at that moment to the instrument that had given life to these epic works; that I was meeting a true renaissance master no less towering than Giotto or Bernini. I guess he knew we were seekers.

He was slight of build, dressed in traditional garb of stovepipe hat, gold crucifix, and long beard. His hands, crossed one over the other in front of him, were a gnarled roadmap of bulging veins, the mark of one who has done much physical labor. His face was serene with black piercing eyes that spoke louder than words. We had no common language and needed none as he proceeded to lead us about his studio, intimating with body language or a tilt of his head how his creative process worked.

At a corner band saw, the only apparent concession to the modern world, he showed how he cut the wood panels and then sanded them. This was followed by the application of multiple, wafer thin sheets of gold leaf, rubbed against his cheek and pressed onto the panel, using only natural body oils as an adhesive. As he did this he closed his eyes and smiled, reminding me of how someone would caress a beloved pet.

A sweep of his hand took us to a low table of hand tied horse hair brushes next to a rainbow selection of pigment jars, all personally ground with stone mortar and pestle. Next he broke an egg, separating the white from the yolk and mixed the yellow with a small dab of water and a dash of pigment, a renaissance technique known as tempera painting employed by old masters such as Titian and long out of vogue due to its delicate nature. With this technique, layer upon layer of thin glazes of paint are applied to the panel, slowly building the luminescent colors that dazzle the viewer as if backlit from within.

Finally he sat before an easel that held a panel with only a pencil sketch on it, motioning for us to join him. With only a few deft brush strokes a smiling Madonna sheltering the infant Christ child in her arms began to take shape. His movements were swift and sure and an enigmatic smile played on his lips as he painted. With his unspoken language of art he revealed the mechanism behind his connection to the Almighty. Everything about this man made me feel that even though he was physically beside us and sharing his creative process, his total being was on an elevated spiritual plane, the art flowing from within him.

The day passed without our noticing as we were as immersed in the work as the good father who would occasionally emit a sigh of pleasure that told us the latest brush stroke had achieved its effect. A sinking sun and growling stomachs announced it was finally time for us to go and as we bid farewell, Father Pefkis bowed his head and said in very halting English, "Go with God"

Father Pefkis and his ancient work technique was an entrée to a time long vanished, a time of imagination and creativity as the world emerged from the sleep of the dark ages and gave birth to the renaissance, and he himself is a direct descendent from that time, the last of a long line of great masters most of whom have gone unnoticed by the world; masters who plied their work for the glory of God and not for public recognition. To visit his studio was to step back five centuries in time.

It makes me wonder if masters such as Titian or Raphael allowed visitors while they worked, and if so, what stories they had to tell.

OF MAN AND BEAST

On the flat icy surface of the northwest Inside Passage, sound skims across the water like a flat stone, distorting distance and betraying those who would move silently through the morning fog.

The blow of several Orcas filters through the mist, and I sense they are near.

It is summer, and transient whales are following schools of Salmon heading north to spawn. In my kayak, I am just one more errant log floating in their domain. It is day six of an eight day paddle off the northeast coast of Canada's Vancouver Island. The waters are full of spawning salmon, and transient Killer Whales are in hot pursuit.

One year ago while paddling near this very spot, I witnessed a pod of Orcas conducting a funeral. The morning was a dull grey and drizzly, as only Alaskan summers can be, and the sky set the mood for what I was to witness.

Fighting my way through bull kelp, I heard the first blow. A large bull led the way, cruising through the mist like an apparition, bearing a stillborn calf across his rostrum. The calf, still bright pink, slumped across his snout like a limp rag, its head and flukes trailing under the surface. The bull moved slowly, not blowing, and five smaller whales followed in single order until they reached deep water in the center of the channel. The bull stopped, holding his silent charge, while the other whales formed around him. The bull slowly lowered his head, and the stillborn whale sank into the depths.

The pain of their loss hung in the air, thicker than the fog.

An old female, most likely the matriarch, lob tailed the water twice, perhaps in silent goodbye, or maybe just a signal that they were finished, but as she did this, all six Orcas came abreast and sounded in unison. They knew I was there and ignored me. That moment was a gift; a point of connection between two species who share the planet, yet rarely meet. It is the silence of a kayak that allows me to enter their world, and whenever I do, I feel the inferior one.

This memory floods over me as the familiar blows reach my ears. I stop paddling and scan the fog bank. They are close.
It is cold this morning and calm. The sun has tried to break through twice without success. The silence is broken only by the cry of a lone eagle taking fish from the littoral. Minnows are jumping; sure sign larger predators are about. My breath hangs visibly white on the air and I zip my fleece up higher.

The calm is broken when a young harbor seal shatters the surface, lunging for my boat and startling me into action. He is clearly terrified, seeking refuge on my bow. In another time and place I might let him rest there, but I sense what is coming and he cannot stay. I slap the water hard, and he veers off, only for a second, but this animal is panic driven and will not be easily deterred.

He approaches a second time and I fend him off with the flat of my blade, watching his pleading eyes as he arches for a final dive. He disappears behind a trail of bubbles.

A brief silver flash passes under my boat, and a second later I am hit square in my floatation vest by a young Salmon. It flops onto my spray skirt, flailing to get back to the water. Then one fish after another begins to strike the side of my boat.

Suddenly, a black dorsal cuts through the fog like a periscope, leaving a white wake, bearing down on me. A quick look around tells me I am surrounded.

The first Orca crosses my bow, lunging as it takes a fish in midair, and before I can react, two more streak past, almost touching me.

The pod is herding a school of Salmon, driving them against a rock wall twenty yards to my port. The pod is arrayed in a semi-circle from twelve to six o'clock around my boat and they have the Salmon cornered. The fish are running in total panic as shiny black fins cut the water like knives, churning it into a crimson red as they take their prey. The Salmon are slamming head first into the wall, knocking themselves senseless. I am in the eye of the storm.

These carnivores have been around my boat on numerous occasions and have always shown themselves to be curious and friendly. To the best of my knowledge there has never been a recorded attack on a man or boat. They are ruthless when it comes to taking prey, yet gentle when in contact with man. Still, I fight the urge to panic and sit in quiet awe as a deadly ballet plays out around me.

I know these are resident whales because the transients only eat mammals, then flash on what a silly thought that is at the moment, since I am a mammal.

A white saddle patch zips under the boat, rolling at the last second to clear my keel while another whale passes parallel, showering me with blow as it moves in for a kill. Glistening dorsals cross left and right, parting the water like torpedoes.

I can feel their clicks and squeals echoing through the fiberglass hull of my boat. They are executing a perfectly coordinated hunt, calling to each other, giving orders, and all of it in spite of my presence.

Salmon lunge in all directions, clearing the water with great leaps. Large black heads break the surface taking fish down from midair. One whale is coming hard, broadside, and I instinctively brace for the crash as he breaks hard left, taking a Salmon as he dives, his backwash causing me to brace hard.

The whales pass within inches, some lightly grazing my boat, but they know where I am and avoid any solid collisions. I sit perfectly still, not wishing to press my luck.

I am soaking wet from blow and covered with bloody scales. Twice, I must brace against the churning, and carefully push a meaty hunk of Salmon off my deck with my paddle blade, not wishing it to tempt a hungry whale. For most of an hour the whales take fish, then gradually, the action slows. They have eaten their fill and I see Dall's Porpoise moving about, taking the few stragglers. Orcas often allow their smaller cousins to join them near the end of a hunt to clean up leftovers.

The final touch is something I have never seen.

Half of the pod forms a single line, parallel to the wall, and turn their flukes toward it. They begin to slowly lob tail, causing waves to break against the rock. They are dislodging the few scared Salmon that have taken refuge in the cracks and crevices while the rest of the whales and the porpoise take down what is left. It is the final act.

In a few moments they go from a feeding frenzy to total lethargy, logging on the surface, gorged and happy like large black sausages surrounding my boat.

The sudden calm allows me to take a headcount and I realize they are all females or juvenile males; not one mature bull among them.

While Orcas are a matriarchal society, it is the alpha bull that stands as protector, and this hunt was sanctioned on his watch. I know he is nearby. I try to imagine where I would place myself as the bodyguard of a dozen feeding whales, and paddle further into the channel to sit and wait him out. Within a minute the tip of his tall black dorsal rises slowly; there is a soft blow that the wind carries towards me in a mist, and I am sitting by the great whale no more than thirty feet away.

He has surfaced gently as a submarine, and his back fin towers over me by five feet. Sunlight twinkles on his ebony back and his saddle patch reflects like an alpine glacier. His dorsal has a slight bend to it and a missing chunk tells me he has met at least one large shark. He is half again as long as my boat and outweighs me by nine tons. He is a flesh eater whose teeth can shred a Great White. I am sitting alone next to the mightiest predator ever to rule the ocean.

He logs on the surface, leisurely, sure of his power, in control of his domain. I am an insignificant interloper, here by his indulgence.

He has not surfaced by chance as he is too wise for this to be a random happening. He chose the time and place to show himself and is now making a statement.

My boat sits between him and his pod; a position he would never allow an enemy to reach. I am not alive by accident for if he thought me a threat to his pod; I would have been the first victim. He knew of my presence long before the hunt began and not only tolerated me, but allowed me to bear witness. I feel this as strongly as if he were talking to me. Perhaps I have been demoted to a curiosity, but I choose to think of it as communication. His black eye, no larger than the tip of my thumb, is fixed on me as I try to fathom the thoughts behind it.

Once again, I feel myself the inferior one, lacking the ability to understand what this animal would tell me.

Fearing to outlast my welcome, I dip my paddle slowly and begin to push away. As I do, the bull moves forward, inching ahead at minimum speed. I paddle a little harder and he is with me, so I dig in and begin to push shovelfuls of water behind me as my bow starts to cut a wake. The bull is pulling away, then senses my frailty and checks his speed, matching mine, even and steady.

His head rises and falls, eye just under the waterline, watching me, urging me on. In my head, I hear him say, "Stay with me." He is allowing me to paddle with him and I take up the challenge. My heart is racing and emotional tears start to cloud my vision.

Even in his lowest gear it is hard for me to keep pace, but I am now part of his pod, and he is my leader, and this will never happen again. I pull my paddle now, abandoning technique, trying to maintain speed. My arms scream with pain but time has slowed. All that matters now is that I stay with this great beast. For a brief time there is nothing but the two of us, moving as one, and if ever an animal gave a gift to man, this is mine. I have no idea how far we have come, but soon can go no further.

I lay my paddle across the cockpit and glide to a halt. I am cold, wet, exhausted, and have never felt more alive. The great whale sees I have stopped and logs a moment, his black eye fixed on me, and then he slowly dives. For a few seconds I am totally alone and the silence is deafening. I look all around and feel very small.

The bull surfaces in the distance where the pod is reforming. He is probably reporting to the matriarch, telling her of the strange creature who entered their space. They turn their flukes toward me and begin to swim. The fog closes slowly and I watch dorsals fade into it like a movie ending, while I sit, sucking air, taking in what has just happened.

I hear the cry of an eagle in the distance and turn my bow towards land to find a home for the night.

LOOKING FOR ERNEST HEMINGWAY

Grand Bahama, while grand, is a tiny speck of Bahamian Island soaked in rum and populated by those searching for a lifestyle that does not always require their presence.

Soon after arriving, I was smitten with the large and beautiful shells known as Conch's. These are the shells you always see bare breasted natives blowing to warn of the impending arrival of white men in the movies. When clean and polished they are very beautiful and sell for a pretty penny all over the Bahamas to tourists dumb enough to pay tourist prices for them.

After seeing what they cost in the stores, I was determined to find my own on the beach no matter how long the search. Lo and behold, no sooner had I set foot on the virgin sand than a Conch was laid at my feet by an incoming wave. The only problem with this Conch is that it still had a live animal inside it. In fact, the animal itself is called a conch and the shell takes its name from its inhabitant. In the Bahamas, Conch is the local delicacy and it is prepared as many ways as Bubba had recipes for Shrimp in Forrest Gump. It is a tasty, white colored mollusk.

Had I not been in such a hurry to procure my own shell I would have discovered the restaurants have giant piles of discarded Conch shell outside in the back all over the island. They are there for the taking. So much for patience.

Now a Conch is not just going to give up its home and slither out because a tourist wants its shell for a souvenir. My Conch in particular had withdrawn deep into the inner recess of its shell and curled up tight in defiance. After prodding and poking to no avail, and convinced that it was making faces at me, I came up with a grand strategy.

Being quite young and stupid at the time, I decided the best way to get the Conch out of the shell was to put it in the shower stall of my condo, plug the drain, and fill the shower with several inches of Lysol. Don't ask why. That is how my juvenile brain worked back then, especially after a liberal lubrication of local rum.

Feeling good that I had outwitted my stubborn mollusk friend and would have my souvenir Conch soon, I departed with my wife on our motorbike for a local bar.

Now this was not just any bar, but a well-used local watering hole known as Harry's.

Back in the old days when Ernest Hemingway used to come to these waters to take a few Marlin, he liked to top off his day by bending an elbow at Harry's. I had to see it while on the island. At first glance, Harry's is nothing more than a shack made of piled palm fronds. It is the history that draws one to this unimpressive establishment.

Inside we were greeted by a tall muscled man the color of deep ebony. Under his tight T-shirt, muscles rippled without moving and he had a gleaming gold tooth in the front of his mouth. His name was Henry, and if I was to typecast a Caribbean bartender, this is the guy I would pick.

I ordered a lager, Irene had a rum fizz, and we asked if he had any Hemingway stories. He laughed and I figured he probably heard that a dozen times a day. He told me he was just a small boy when Hemingway frequented this bar, but his father knew the man. In fact his father has boxed with Ernest.

I had heard stories of how Hemingway, when in his cups, would slam a $100 dollar bill on the bar and challenge any man to go three minutes with him, bare knuckles. There were few takers, but occasionally someone was willing. Ernest usually used the money to buy a round for the house after thrashing his opponent. I had heard of a very large Mulatto in Cuba who supposedly fought himself to a bloody draw, but had no notion of anyone ever having beaten Hemingway. His ability with his fists was only rivaled by his skill with the pen. Of course it was also this very pen that helped to enhance the reputation.

Henry told me his father had not only gone the three minutes with Hemingway but had beaten him. A good story, but who knows? Certainly I was not the one to challenge it and a good story was what I had come for. In fact if Henry's father looked anything like his son, I have no doubts he could have beaten Hemingway.

Then Henry pointed to a large glass container high on a shelf behind the bar and asked me if I knew what it was. The container appeared to be about two liters tall and full of a yellow liquid. My first thought was one I cared not to share, but when Henry read my mind, he nodded his head yes and laughed out loud.

When he laughed his muscles rippled, his gold tooth caught the light and suddenly I felt as though Ernest was right there in the room.

He told me that after his father had beaten Hemingway, Ernest, not to be outdone, produced another $100 bill and offered it to the man who could out do him with eliminating liquid waste from his body.

Apparently there were several takers for this one, being mostly full of rum and ready to do it anyway for free, not to mention not having to get beat up in the process. Several containers were produced, money was laid out, for side betting was inevitable at this point, and a crowd gathered around the bar, as various manly members both famous and infamous were brought forth.

The contest began with men straining and groaning. One by one they finished their task, until only Henry's father and Ernest were still producing. Finally Henry's father was done but Hemingway kept going and going like the energizer bunny.

When he finished, the container was full and no one could doubt who the most prodigious water maker was. Hemingway again bought a round for the house and staggered off into history. The immense results of his output were preserved in the very jar in question before me now and have sat there ever since.

At least that is the story Henry told me. We finished our drinks, thanked him for his time, and left to ponder the validity of his story. I decided on my ride back to the condo that if the story was true, it was certainly a great one, and if not, I would have been proud to have made it up. Even if it held nothing other than colored water, that container was worth thousands of drinks over countless hours.

When we got back to our condo an angry landlord confronted us.

It seems the housekeeper had entered in our absence and screamed when she found a dead Conch lying inside the shower stall.

A LIFE WITHOUT DREAMS

At 67 Natalia still held a slight veneer of beauty which was most unusual for a post war child of Russia.

From a distance she looks younger than her years but it always the hands that always betray ones age.

The day we met in Saint Petersburg, through a mutual friend, she insisted on taking me to the Tikhvin cemetery, a maze of gigantic baroque monuments to famous dead Russians. At the grave of Pushkin's wife, she closed her eyes, apparently transported to another place, and in the softest of voices, began to recite his poetry, obviously imprinted on her soul as it seems to be in that of most Russians.

Even though we had just met I felt her need to talk to someone from another place; someone whose life was not molded by the past shackles of Communism, and there, among the elite artistic deceased of her country, her life story poured out like a bursting dam.

It began with a tirade against the just re-elected president Putin, whom it seemed had no support from anyone I met in the entire country and had apparently stolen the recent election as everyone had predicted he would. "We are now free to say anything we want," she told me, "But life is just the same." Still she could not help giving me a running commentary on Russian history that that also flowed from most of my local acquaintances, realizing that those of her age received more political indoctrination than education as children.

As we strolled past the graves of Russia's great writers she spoke of how her mother told her as a young girl to never have dreams as they would never come true, and that she should get a job as a waitress or cook because that way she would always have food. This was the mind set of those who survived the war, living on garbage or starving. She said this as a matter of fact with no self- pity in her voice, making the gap obvious between those who grew up under communism and the young girls strolling by in their short skirts and high heels wobbling over cobblestone streets with I –pods in their ears.

I changed the conversation and told her I had a small amount of ashes with me; the remains of a deceased friend whose final wish was to be spread all over the world, wherever his friends traveled, and I thought this a proper place to leave them. This was obviously not a mood raiser and a look of incomprehension spread across her face as she asked me what I meant.

I told her about my friend, a famous man and world traveler whose friends were spreading his ashes wherever we now traveled, but could see that she didn't understand. "Why do you have human ashes?" she asked. "Bodies only burn in war." I explained as best as I could, but apparently cremation is an alien concept in Russia and she said I could not do that there, meaning the grave of Mrs. Pushkin, and made me feel as though it would be some sort of desecration. I did not pursue the matter and we walked on a while, not speaking until we reached the grave of Tolstoy where she paused and said, "OK, you can leave ashes here." Obviously Mr. Tolstoy was much further down her list of great people.

She would not speak of her childhood anymore but told me of various jobs she held as a young woman, trying to keep food on the table for her mother and herself after losing her father to the "Great Patriotic War."

Her eyes finally showed some life when she told me she now runs a bed and breakfast for exchange students and they bring the world to her for the first time. She pulled out a photo of a girl from Ghana and said, "Imagine seeing Ghana" as though it were another planet. I told her that now she was traveling the world through the eyes of her boarders and that in itself was living a dream. She looked thoughtful for a moment, obviously considering this concept for the first time and with a tiny smile said, "You're right." We walked on in silence as I processed this incredible insight to a culture long alien to me.

My childhood included the days of bomb shelters, and drop and cover drills in school, living in constant fear of when the "Rooskies" would drop the big one directly on top of my house. I remember the Cuban missile crisis as though it were yesterday, was taught that communism was a dirty word, and now I was learning from their side, from a parallel life that was raised on the same stories about America. But we were mainly separated by the fact that I grew up in a land not knowing hunger or living in fear that my government would knock on my door in the middle of the night. We parted ways at the underground station, and she invited my wife and I to her home the next day, "for pancakes" she said, as I watched her descend into the bowls of Saint Petersburg.

Irene and I both knew what a rare opportunity this invitation was but showed up without expectations. We arrived by cab to find an unkempt gray complex with a dark crumbling staircase that seemed typical of public dwelling, left over from Soviet days when the state assigned people a home. It's location, less than a mile from the fortress of Peter the Great, implied that Natalia was better off than the average local citizen.

The rooms were tiny as expected, as was her husband who was unexpected, because I had been told he was rarely around. She introduced us and immediately began to point out her wall of photos of relatives, all in military uniform; all from the "Great War" that was still her preoccupation. The apartment told me more about her life than she did, small and spare; the only decorations being photos of relatives and plastic flowers. The credenza, aside from the enormous television that seemed an altar to Glasnost, was filled with books on Russian history and photos of her husband with various people unknown to me. Tiny figurines of Lenin, and Yuri Gagarin, sat next to a line of American movie DVD's.

From the window I looked over the bleak gray neighborhoods created under Lenin and Stalin, at the towering golden spire of Peter's fortress, a constant reminder of the divided classes.

She seated us on the sofa in front of the gigantic LG screen, and proceeded to show Irene a photo album of her boarders from around the world, obviously a source of great pride to her. Her husband who spoke only a few words of English then popped in a DVD and we spent the next half hour watching endless expanses of ice and barren ocean because it was a personal video of his former work as an engineer on a Soviet ice breaker in the far north. The one entertaining moment came when it showed crew members tossing cans of condensed milk to the polar bears that exploded when they bit into them.

While the bears crunched cans, Natalia disappeared into the tiny kitchen and finally called us to eat. The meal was thinly sliced strips of fresh local trout, bright pink and served raw, covered with chopped scallions

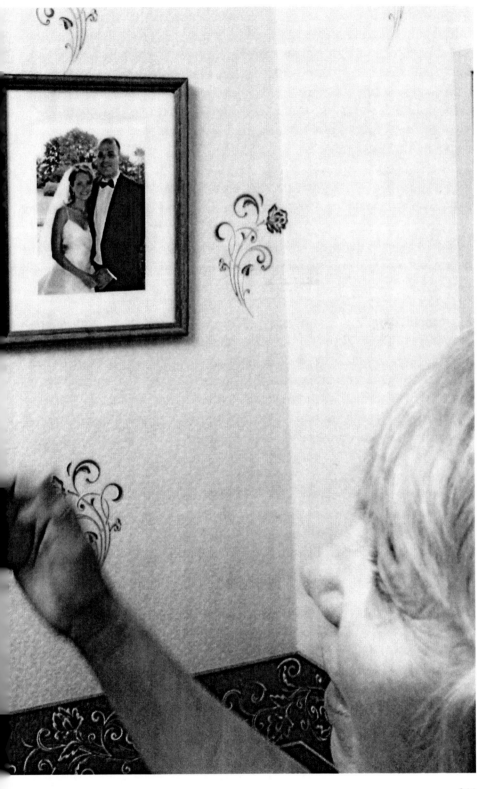

that tasted just like very salty lox. While Natalia produced dozens of tiny round pancakes, her husband would plop dollops of sour cream on them and then filled our shot glasses with vodka as we participated in the most important ceremony in daily Russian life, tossing back shot after shot, and with each one, offering a toast to whatever common ground came to mind. Russians drink vodka like water and to not do so is to offend them. By my fifth shot I think I was toasting the television screen as the day's events began to blur.

When she asked about my work she could not understand making money as a travel writer, saying, "Who would pay for this?" and after my lengthy description of what I do she said, "No wonder America is so rich." My efforts to explain that I was not wealthy, but a working writer who had to hustle to make a living, fell on deaf ears. To her anyone who could afford to travel was very rich.

I commented on how scantily clad I thought the women of Saint Petersburg were in the frigid wind that sweeps in from the gulf of Finland, and how brazenly forward they seemed, openly flirting with me even while I was with my wife, and this made her laugh. She said that the mentality of most Russian women was to marry a rich foreigner; anyone not Russian, and to move away. This explained why the young girls looked like Vogue models while their temporary local boyfriends dressed like homeless lumberjacks.

I came away from Russia with the belief that there are really only two classes, the very rich who made fortunes in the black market after the collapse of the Soviet union and still run the country through intimidation, and the very poor, who were left behind by a corrupt government that cares nothing for its people in its relentless pursuit of power.

Natalia seemed to be one of the few left in between, leading a rather nice life by local standards, but always wondering what might have been. People no longer cringe at the mention of the KGB. Now it is called the Federal Security Force and seems to be on a somewhat shorter leash, but big brother is still listening if its subjects step too far out of line. My time with Natalia was an open window that answered many questions about a society long closed to most of the world.

There is no true ending to this story yet as Mr. Putin assumed another six years of power, apparently against the will of the majority, and if he leaves then, he will have ruled for 16 years.

Some would call that a dictatorship, but in Russia it is simply life.

AUTHOR'S CODA

Introducing the modern world to the old one and vice versa has always been a fine line for explorers to tread no matter how small the intrusion. I readily admit to mixed feelings of guilt about many of my trips. Part of me wants these societies to remain as they are, private, untouched by the outside world. And yet the part of me that put them into this book wants to share them with everyone.

In the end, the old saying of "Take only photos and leave only footprints" does not go far enough, as even the footprints will at some point make a difference. Those of us who wander afar must always bear in mind the fact that everything we bring with us, including our physical presence, has the potential of altering the status quo of where we are visiting. As people continue to venture farther off the beaten path they inevitably bring outside influences that can have negative effects on less developed societies. As the world continues to shrink, and cultures collide, it is inevitable that we will all assimilate something from others into our own in a glacially slow process of becoming one world. The question travelers must ask themselves is how responsible do they want to be for the pace of that process?

Remote travel is not for everyone, but the curiosity of what is out there should be.

If this book has taken you to places you could not or would not go and given any food for thought, then it is a success.

ABOUT THE AUTHOR

James Michael Dorsey is an explorer, author, artist, photographer, and lecturer, who has traveled extensively in 44 countries. His principle interest is documenting remote cultures in Africa and Asia.

He is a correspondent for Camerapix International and has written for Colliers, United Airlines, The BBC, The Christian Science Monitor, Los Angeles Times, Natural History, Vagabundo, WEND, Sea Kayaker, Perceptive Travel, Seattle Times, Orlando Sentinel, Chicago Tribune, and TravelersTales book series, plus several in flight magazines of African airlines. His first book is entitled, Tears, Fear, and Adventure, and his work has appeared in five separate anthologies.

His photography is represented by SHUTTERSTOCK and CAMERAPIX Intl. and has been featured by the Smithsonian.com, the National Wildlife Federation and International Whaling Commission. His work has twice been chosen as Kodak Internationals' "Photo of the Day." He has appeared on National Public Radios' "Weekend America" program. He is a Fellow of the Explorers Club and a former director of the Los Angeles Adventurer's Club

www.jamesdorsey.com

ABOUT THE PUBLISHER

Vagabundo Magazine was established in 2011 by adventurer Brendan van Son. The magazine focuses on telling the tales of places far off the beaten path and of people whose stories deserve to be written.

Far from the mainstream, Vagabundo Magazine focuses on the world as it is, not as seen through the rose-coloured glasses of mainstream writers nor the fear-inducing picture often painted by the media.

The stories told by James Dorsey in these pages teach readers of our travel mantra, which is to travel not for bragging rights, but as a way of carrying and passing on information about the world as we see it. We are global citizens and travelers first and foremost. We are publishers only to help facilitate the words told by special people like James, and to insure they inspire others to take on the same challenge as he has done.

www.vagabundomagazine.com

Lightning Source UK Ltd.
Milton Keynes UK
UKOW03f0702280417

300091UK00001B/33/P